VOCAL PRODUCTION & RECORDING

Berklee Press

Jeannie Gagné
Prince Charles Alexander

To access audio visit:
www.halleonard.com/mylibrary
Enter Code
1918-3128-1314-5834

BERKLEE PRESS

Editor in Chief: Jonathan Feist

Senior Vice President Pre-College, Online, and Professional Programs/
CEO and Cofounder of Berklee Online: Debbie Cavalier

RECORDINGS: Vocal Tracks

Soprano: Jeannie Gagné

Alto: Adyana Luna

Tenor: Mikey Mousaw

Bass/Baritone: Tom Baskett

Recording Engineer: Gerson Lazo-Quiroga

ISBN 978-0-87639-232-4

1140 Boylston Street
Boston, MA 02215-3693 USA
(617) 747-2146

Visit Berklee Press Online at
www.berkleepress.com

Study music online at
online.berklee.edu

Distributed By

Visit Hal Leonard Online
www.halleonard.com

Berkleee Press, a publishing activity of Berklee College of Music, is a not-for-profit educational publisher.
Available proceeds from the sales of our products are contributed to the scholarship funds of the college.

CONTENTS

ACKNOWLEDGMENTS

FROM JEANNIE GAGNÉ

To my family, dear friends, and colleagues. Thank you for your incredible support and inspiration. I learn a great deal from you. To my beloved children, Arianna and Dylan. My mother Molly's light continues to shine and guide me; she helped me edit my first book, and I believe she has been with me in some way for this one, as well. My fathers Cris and Paul, you are always in my heart. To my brothers, Dr. David Gagné and Stephen Gagné, and Dr. Jim Gagné (RIP) may your journey in the stars be fascinating. To Danai Gagné, my sister, I am sure your musical light shines in heaven. To Melia Gagné Giuffo. To Lance Dieter, Ana Guigui, Bernadette Drayton, Deb Lynch, Andrea Capozzoli, Alizon Lissance, Cassandre McKinley, Gabrielle Goodman, Donna McElroy, Nichelle Mungo, Dr. Elizabeth Bennett, and Dr. Kathleen Howland. To Rick and Cindy Benard, Kimberly French and Michael Rozyne, Stan Strickland, and Bernard Drayton. To Voice Chair Anne Peckham and Assistant Chair Phil Lima for their support. There are so many additional esteemed fellow faculty in the Voice Department at Berklee College of Music whom I am also inspired and humbled by; you are a remarkable group of talented, caring, and supportive teachers.

And of course to my cowriter Prince Charles Alexander: your genius, caring, patience, and good humor have made collaborating on this book a delight. And a huge thank you to our stalwart editor Jonathan Feist.

To my students in the U.S., in China, in Europe, in South America, in Mexico, and in so many other places; and to my students at Berklee College of Music, and Berklee Online. You inspire me every day, and I learn a great deal from you, too. Your passions for learning have helped me to shape this book, and continue to make teaching a true joy.

To my muses Joni Mitchell, Chaka Khan, Ella Fitzgerald, Bonnie Raitt, Sarah Vaughan, Whitney Houston, Abraham Adzenyah, Peter Gabriel, Stevie Wonder, Stevie Ray Vaughan, Cheryl Crow—just to name a few who have inspired my creativity since I began songwriting and singing as a child. To my piano teacher Jeaneane Dowis (RIP), and voice teachers Shirley Meier (RIP), Victoria Clark, Kathryn Wright, and Mark Baxter. To jazz, funk, gospel, soul, singer-songwriter, folk, and the blues: you keep me going. And always, thank you to the Universal Light for your eternal guidance and inspiration. My deepest gratitude.

And lastly, to my readers. Thank you for your endless enthusiasm and desire to grow as a musician, vocalist, producer, recordist, entrepreneur. May this book help inspire your music and productions to be well seen and well heard.

FROM PRINCE CHARLES ALEXANDER

The Immediate Family: Candice, Chloe, and Aden Alexander; Katrina, Khemis, Kailynn, Karon and Rico Jackson; Romeo, Caroline, and Josephine Alexander; and Marie Alexander (RIP Mum).

More Family: Catherine and John Wideman; Bruce and Doyon Purse; Theresa Griffith; Remy Fisher; Adella Gautier, Tiffany Chase, Amber and August Zu-Johnson, Annie, Sheila, Joel, Lisa, Pam, and Michael Talbert; Jose and Angela Ramos; Charles and Dolores Snow; Eileen Jordan; and all my extended family descended from Julia Watson Dailey Gautier Lee (Mama).

The Muses: Larry "Maurice Starr" Johnson, Michael "Kashif Saleem" Jones, Conant "Tony" Rose, the remaining members of the City Beat Band (Marilyn and Marlene Muldrow, CL Kelly, Tomas Doncker, Darryll Mull, Kim Davis, Greg Barrett, Alix Anthony), Jodeci, Usher, Mary J. Blige, Missy Elliott, Faith Evans, Cheryl "Salt" James, Rufus Blaq, Chad "Dr. Ceuss" Elliott, Catherine Ringer and Les Rita Mitsouko, IAM, Destiny's Child, Angie Stone, Luther Vandross, Stokley Williams, Carl Thomas, Lance Alexander, Horace Brown, Frederick "Toots" Hibbert, Gordon Chambers, Donnie McClurkin, Hank Shocklee, and Elai Tubo.

The Interviewees: Manny Marroquin, Ebonie Smith, Neal H. Pogue, Marcella Araica, Derek Ali, Stuart White, John Kercy, Young Guru, Bryan-Michael Cox, Simone Torres, Leslie Brathwaite, Ann Mincieli, Martina Albano, Speech (*Arrested Development*), Shanti Das, Jason Orr, Leslie Gaston-Bird, James P. Nichols, Maty Mzurek, Jeff Jedi Jones, Angela Piva, Jon Fausty (RIP), Luis Saldarriaga, Michael Brauer, Will Wells, Tyler Scott, Taurees Habib, and Trevor Horn.

Thanks also to: Carl Beatty, Rob Jaczko, Dan Thompson, and Barbara Thomas at Berklee College of Music; Debbie Cavalier and Boriana Alexiev at Berklee Online; Dan Godfrey, Hilary Poriss, and Dr. Doug Bielmeier at Northeastern University.

It has been such a pleasure to co-write with Jeannie Gagné. Her passion, inspiration, amazing ability, and sense of musical community shine brightly within every page of this book. Thank you Jonathan Feist for your nerves of steel and gentle prodding. You are amazing.

INTRODUCTION

This book is intended for people who are creating vocal-focused recording projects. You may be recording and producing vocalists, self-producing your own vocals, or you may simply wish to improve your producing and recording skills.

To get the most out of the book, we recommend having some experience with a DAW (Digital Audio Workstation), which will save you time as you work through this book and apply its concepts to your productions. There are several available on the market, for example: Logic Pro X (Apple), Live (Ableton), Studio One (PreSonus), Pro Tools (Avid), FL Studio (Image Line), Cubase (Steinberg), Audacity (The Audacity Team), and GarageBand (Apple). Note that some of these programs are more complex than others, and all take time to learn, so please refer to the user manual, and/or YouTube how-to videos, to gain a basic understanding of your DAW.

It is best to pre-create an area in your home or work space that is ready to go with a few clicks of a button. As much as you are able, make it easy and quick to begin recording each day. This will enable you to get right into your creative process, and an efficient work space is a productive work space.

ABOUT THE AUDIO

To access the accompanying audio, go to www.halleonard.com/mylibrary and enter the code found on the first page of this book. This will grant you instant access to every example. Examples with accompanying audio are marked with an audio icon.

Please note that many computers have three built-in speakers: left, right, and a subwoofer. On MacBook computers, when you are listening back to the book's audio examples over your computer speakers, if you pan right, you will hear sounds through the right speaker. However, if you pan left, you will hear both the left speaker and the subwoofer, making the sound appear to be in the center. Therefore, because many of the audio examples that describe panning left, right, and center, we recommend that you use headphones, and/or studio reference monitors, for optimal listening.

CHAPTER 1

The Magic Triangle: Vocalist, Producer, and Recordist

Producing a song begins with an idea that could be a musical groove, a vocal melody, or lyrics on a napkin. There are three tasks that must be accomplished when you are recording vocals for a song. One is performing the vocal. Second is creating an intended experience for the listener. Third is recording the vocal well enough to service the intended experience. Mitch Benoff, a colleague and Berklee College of Music vocal production professor, labels this relationship "The Magic Triangle." The roles of the Magic Triangle are:

- **Vocalist.** Executes the vocal performance of the song and collaborates with the producer.
- **Producer.** Manages the creative/artistic experience of the song, and has business functions.
- **Recordist.** Captures, edits, and mixes the vocal performances of the song.

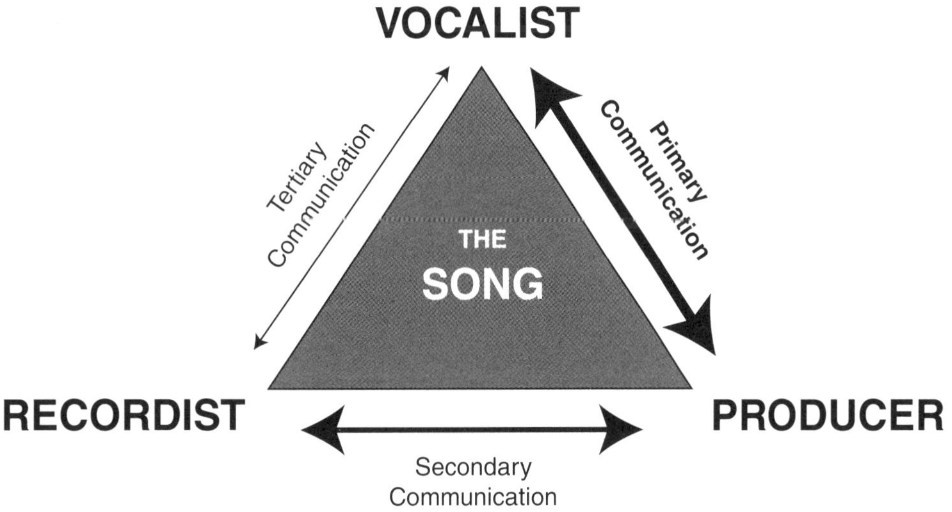

FIG. 1.1. The Magic Triangle

The Magic Triangle can be three people, two people, or one person, depending on the project. But even with one person, each of these roles is present. Viewing the vocal recording and production process as three distinct roles that are part of a collaborative process allows greater insight into delivering excellent and highly productive work each time you record.

The producer is the objective voice, the vocalist is the subjective voice, and the recordist is the technical voice. The vocalist may have attachment to the performance, where the producer is ideally looking at the project from a larger lens and is attached to the overall objective of the project. The recordist's focus is on recording practices that meet the needs of the producer and the vocalist.

VOCALIST

The vocalist is at the top of the Magic Triangle. This "division of labor" model allows the vocalist to focus primarily on the execution of vocal ideas. As we will see throughout the book, important considerations for the vocalist include preparation, vocal skills, studio environment, and the overall goal of the project. The environment of a well-run session should be as comfortable as possible for the vocalist to support finding their "zone of creativity." Included in this zone is great communication with their producer and recordist team during the recording session.

Types of Vocalists

We address you the producer, the recordist (recording engineer), and the vocalist in this book. There are many types of vocalists whose performances can be produced and recorded:

singer — a musician whose instrument is voice, with an ability to sing a melody, with or without musical accompaniment

lead singer — a singer who performs the primary melody of the song, may also sing featured improvisational lines, and is placed "on top" of the mix in order to be heard clearly

artist — a branded personality who sings, and/or raps, performing their own songs or songs written by other songwriters who work within their brand

professional singer — a singer who is hired for someone else's project as the lead vocalist and/or background vocalist, and may be skilled in a variety of styles

background vocalist — a singer who works within a group setting to blend, harmonize, and match the vocal quality and phrasing of the lead singer

singer-songwriter — a singer who writes their own songs, and often self-accompanies on piano, guitar, or another instrument

rapper — a vocalist with an ability to perform lyrics using complex rhythms, may sing melodies, and performs with or without musical accompaniment

spoken word artist a poet whose instrument is voice, with an ability to perform text with or without musical accompaniment

speaker a vocalist who records their own work, such as a comedian, a professional orator, a book actor or narrator

voice or dialogue actor a vocalist who records the voice of a character, such as for animation or an audio book, or who records "automated dialogue replacement" (ADR) for films in place of the original actor, such as when an original line was spoken incorrectly, removing foul language, or overdubbing in a different language

PRODUCER

The primary communication within the Magic Triangle for the vocalist is with the producer. The secondary communication within the Magic Triangle for the producer is the recordist. The producer serves to streamline communication within the Magic Triangle, as shown in the figure 1.1 illustration. This is much more efficient and less confusing for the vocalist, who will already have enough to occupy their creative focus. Discussed in advance, the creative goals for the song are in the hands of the producer, who understands what is being delivered by the vocalist and how it's being captured by the recordist. The producer's communication should be one of trust and collaboration, while serving the needs of the project.

Different producers will develop this relationship based on how they connect with their vocalists. For instance, some vocalists prefer to perform the entire song before discussing their performance with the producer. Others prefer to perform a section of the song, such as a verse or a chorus, before discussing it with the producer. And yet other singers like to perfect each line of the song as they go along, in constant consultation with the producer. The producer's ability to deliver cogent and encouraging feedback during the vocal recording will make or break the session, which can eventually make or break the song.

RECORDIST

Secondary communication between the recordist and the producer covers technical aspects of the session such as track count, reverb settings, and EQ. A third, or tertiary, communication can occur directly between the recordist and the vocalist. This communication might be about technical and sonic matters, including the choice of microphone, the headphone mix, the positioning of the vocalist in the room, mic placement, and even the mood lighting of the session.

In some sessions, one person may be both producer and recordist, or in the case of self-producing, one person may perform all three roles.

HOW THE MAGIC TRIANGLE WORKS

The Magic Triangle begins during the preproduction process. Preproduction is the preparation phase before a recording. It provides an opportunity to arrive at a shared vision between producer and vocalist prior to the recording session(s). Preproduction includes details like song selection, musical goals and vision, schedule, hiring the players, choosing the recording space, and making sure the budget is on track. Preproduction could entail a brief phone conversation or an extended meeting over a period of hours or days. It can include discussing and listening to music that you both like, considering several songs, and determining which song to record first. It can include deciding where you will record—whether you record simultaneously with a band or with a prerecorded track. Budget may be discussed, as well as how many hours the project will take, how many hours to work in a day, who beyond the Magic Triangle is invited to be present during the sessions, and when to take breaks. The preproduction process is an efficient way to get the creative juices flowing while ensuring that everyone is on board with the same vision and vibe.

Let's look at some examples.

Scenario 1: A One-Person Recording Session

When you're acting as all three team members in one—vocalist, producer, and recordist—you need to segment yourself into different roles during the recording process. Your goal is to be objective as the producer, skilled as the recordist, and inspired as the vocalist. In the beginning stages, allow yourself to create from a place free of judgment. This is essential so you don't cut off your creative inspiration. Write/produce your songs with unfettered creativity, then come back to edit them later. This can be a challenging balance to strike, and is true whether or not you are a hobbyist or pro musician.

Scenario 2: A Two-Person Recording Session

When two people collaborate on a recording session, they are sharing the three Magic Triangle roles. For example:

- the vocalist/producer works with a producer/recordist
- the vocalist/producer works with a recordist (who does not offer production advice)
- the vocalist (who does not produce the session) works with a producer/recordist

Both people agree ahead of time about their roles for the session, keeping the vision, vibe, and goals for the session in mind during the process.

Scenario 3: A Three-Person Recording Session

When three people collaborate on a recording session, the Magic Triangle roles are more clearly defined. The vocalist provides the performance, the producer is responsible for the project's vision, and the recordist manages the technology. The roles don't have to be exclusive, e.g., the vocalist could offer production ideas, the producer could offer technical advice, and the recordist could suggest performance stylings. However, the most effective results occur when each one stays primarily in their own lane.

Scenario 4: A Vocalist for Hire

In the previous three scenarios, the vocalist may be involved in both the creation and performance of the work. In Scenario 4, the vocalist is hired to perform for a project.

In this scenario, a producer or songwriter directs the project, and may or may not hire a recordist. The vocalist's job is to learn the song, and provide the performance that best brings the song to life. This scenario works best when the directions, vision, vocal qualities, and vibe are all clearly communicated to the vocalist.

CONVERSATION AND COLLABORATION

What is the secret sauce for a successful project? It is no secret at all. It begins with conversation. In the spirit of collaboration, everyone should be on board with the goals of the project. As simple as it sounds, the language you use will have an effect on the session. Positive language will keep the session flowing, while negative language can stunt creativity and collaboration.

Empowerment Sandwich

Positive reinforcement, when balanced with corrections, works better than pure negative feedback for getting results. The empowerment sandwich (or compliment sandwich) originated in the 1940s and was purportedly popularized by Mary Kay Ash (Mary Kay Cosmetics) as a way to balance critique with encouragement.

It is commonly used today in three parts:

1. Describe something very positive about the performer's effort.
2. Provide the critique of the effort; then,
3. Describe another thing that is positive about the performer's effort.

In this way, you are both supporting the person's efforts without "throwing them under the bus," while pointing out clearly what needs to be worked on or done differently. This technique places a critique in between positive opening and closing comments, like putting food in between two slices of bread.

For vocal producing, empowerment sandwich language might sound something like this:

1. **Opening:** "That was a great take with lots of passion!"
2. **Critique:** "The third word was a bit under the desired pitch."
3. **Closing:** "But, you covered it so well it still feels like a great candidate for the final vocal comp."

And then seal the sandwich with, "Let's record another to see if the performance can become even more magical."

Critiquing eloquently in this manner can take practice, especially when topics like breathing, posture, articulation, pitch, projection, mic distance, register shifts, timbral variations, vibrato, and attitude or vibe are so personal to the vocalist. But, doing so helps to build and nurture the shared vision.

The hierarchical communication of the Magic Triangle also helps to avoid too many voices barking instructions at the vocalist while they are in the recording booth focusing on their performance. When each participant is efficient with the unique skills they bring to the session, the workflow runs more smoothly and productively.

Our scenarios for vocalist, producer, and recordist communication are, of course, a goal state. Keeping track of the separate roles can be challenging to navigate for any of our scenarios. The vocalist wants to focus on performance. The producer wants to focus on the big picture and a project that will be received well. The recordist wants to make sure that all technical considerations run smoothly and efficiently. With practice, you can become skilled at collaborative communication for any or all of these roles within the Magic Triangle.

What happens if the team faces challenges?

There are some common, real-life scenarios that can, unfortunately, hamper the team spirit—or worse, kill a project. In one scenario, the vocalist is a singer-songwriter who brings their project to a producer with a great reputation, who in turn hires a recordist. This is very common. The vocalist pays the producer to make their song sound killer, and the producer pays the recordist for their technical skill. The producer and recordist may see their roles like animators working on a film, drawing each action slide to bring the animated characters to life, in which the vocalist is one of the characters.

This is a perfect setup for a clash of wills, in which the vocalist feels that while they're paying for a different level of expertise than what they could have provided on their own, it's still their baby. Meanwhile, the producer/recordist wants to put their name on a product that reflects their creative vision and expertise, which is now their baby. If these two visions don't align, and the communication breaks down, the best solution is to pause the session or take a break. Speak with one another and check in with how everyone's doing. Go back to review and restate the agreed upon goals for the session. It could even be as simple as needing a short rest, or time to eat a snack!

When the vocalist feels comfortable with the team, and trusts their judgment—and when the producer and recordist respect the vocalist—the working relationship can yield a magical recording.

In chapter 2, we begin deconstructing the process of creating a magical recording using vocal production tools. Our first tool is vocal arranging.

CHAPTER 2

Vocal Arranging

Arranging vocals has been around since before recorded sound. In 1877, Thomas Edison's invention of the phonograph allowed the human voice to be captured on a fixed medium. The phonograph used a megaphone-shaped device both to record sound and play it back. Fast-forward to the early 1950s, guitarist Les Paul invented the first multi-track recording device. His magnetic tape machine enabled multiple vocal performances to be recorded onto the same song at different times. You can hear this technique in the song "How High the Moon," by Les Paul and Mary Ford (1951).

Stereo sound was yet another invention of the 1950s that gave us two playback speakers to listen to, instead of one. It's adoption gave the vocal arranger a wider sonic spectrum for the lead and background vocals to occupy. Over the decades this use of the stereo field has moved from magnetic tape, to digital tape, to your present-day DAW.

Today, most popular songs are arranged within a DAW using a combination of musical choices and sonic placement within the stereo field. For example, you could arrange three-part harmony background vocals (a musical choice) that are panned to the center of the stereo field, or that are panned to the left and right sides of the stereo field (a sonic choice).

Anytime you have more than one lead vocal in a recording, you are creating a vocal arrangement. A vocal arrangement can add unison, harmony, counterpoint, and a rich sonic quality to songs. It can be any combination of voices, such as a duo, a trio, or a chorus; doubled harmonies, double-tracked lead vocals; or multitracked background parts that weave around the lead vocal. You can use spoken word or "whisper tracks" to add special effects.

SONG GENRE AND STYLES

While there is no clear way to define every genre and subgenre in today's global market, you will find commonalities of form and style between songs that are similarly labeled by genre, even though they are reaching out to different demographic markets.

One great way to find songs with vocal production ideas that you can model for your project's genre is by referencing published song lists in the style you're producing. *Billboard Magazine* has been the leading reference for songs in a wide variety of genres since 1936. There are several other publications and online sites that provide lists of songs, based on search parameters such as style, recording artist, and era. You can also visit streaming websites and services to learn which songs use interesting vocal production techniques within a genre. Listen closely to what arrangers and vocalists have done before to learn how they employ arranging aspects such as vocal tone, registration, stacking vocals, timing, diction, vibrato or straight tone, long or short notes, and call-and-response.

Let's take a closer look at some of the vocal arranging techniques that you may have heard in songs you listen to every day.

VISUALIZING THE SONG

The lead vocal is the focal point of your song. The role of the vocal producer and arranger is to guide the vocalist towards the best performance for the song.

The first technique is going over the lyrics with the vocalist, which they should know and understand very well. This will maximize the intention of their performance. Sit with the vocalist to map out which lyrics provide the strongest and clearest visualization for the song's emotional content. The vocalist can make notes on their music, practicing which words to stress within their phrasing.

In this example (listen to audio track 1), notice how the lyrical meaning changes depending on which word is stressed, illustrated in capital letters.

The **CHILD** ran down the hill. (i.e., not an adult)

The child **RAN** down the hill. (i.e., didn't walk)

1 The child ran **DOWN** the hill. (i.e., not up)

The child ran down the **HILL.** (i.e., not the pathway)

Another technique is for you to suggest that the vocalist imagines the song playing out like a movie in front of them while they perform it. They focus their eyes forward as they sing, in order to imagine the story as it unfolds. Who are the characters? What is the location? What colors are strongest in the scene? Is it day, or night? Sunny, or rainy? Winter, or summer? What are they wearing, and what are the other characters wearing? Is it indoors, or outdoors? How do they feel as that character, physically? Encourage them to use their arms to reach out to the characters or scene in this imaginary movie, while allowing their body to move some so they're not standing stiffly at the microphone. When they visualize what they're singing about clearly, using their body comfortably for expression—while being aware of their proximity to the microphone—their performance can be taken to a more engaging level.

STORYBOARD MAPPING

It can be helpful to map out how the lead vocal will be performed in your song before you record. Even if sheet music provides the arrangement, a storyboard format can be helpful to visualize the big picture. Storyboards are used in film production to depict how a scene will look, frame-by-frame. Using this concept for your song, you can map out line-by-line how the lead vocal will begin, develop, and conclude. What dynamics are you using? Registers? Vocal qualities? Are the lyrics sung more like you would speak them, or more melodious? What words are you accenting for lyrical interpretation?

Here are examples of storyboards to help you visualize adding harmonies or other vocal parts. It is built around the song form. You can do this either with text, or by creating a visual map such as these. (Vox is a common abbreviation for "voice" or "vocals.")

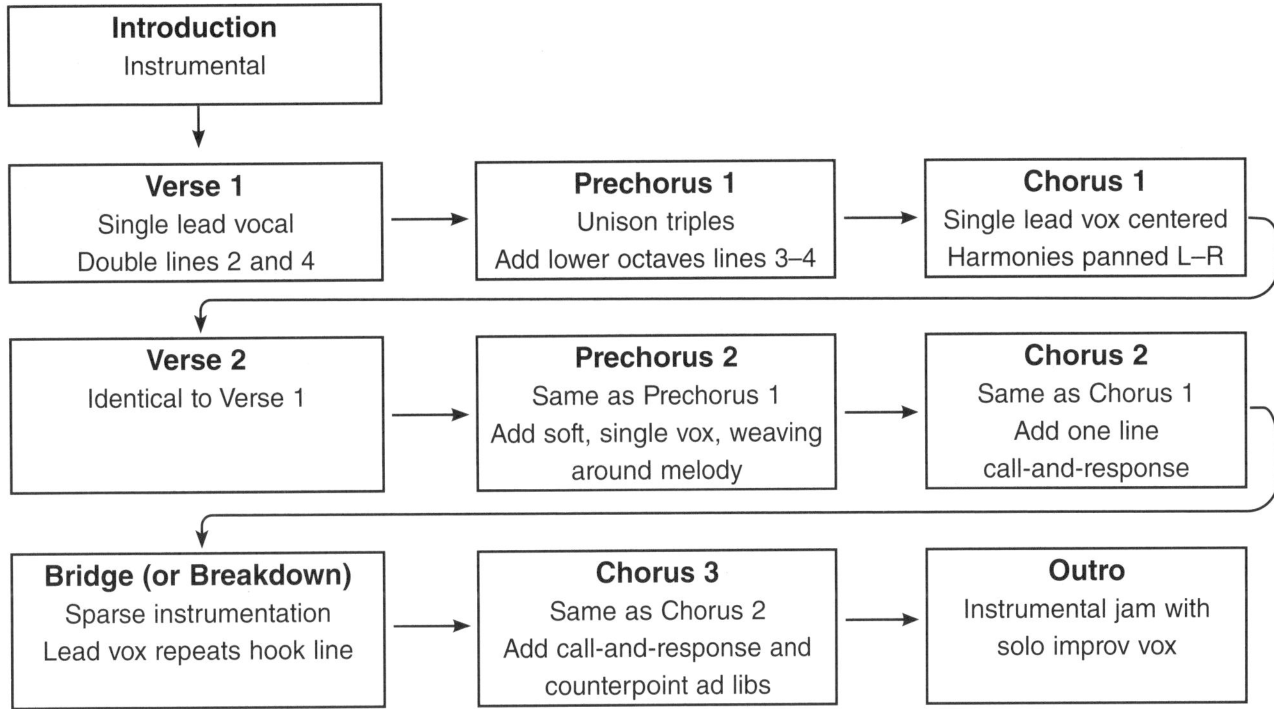

FIG. 2.1. Storyboard Example for a Pop Song

Here's an example storyboard for a pop song with a rap feature.

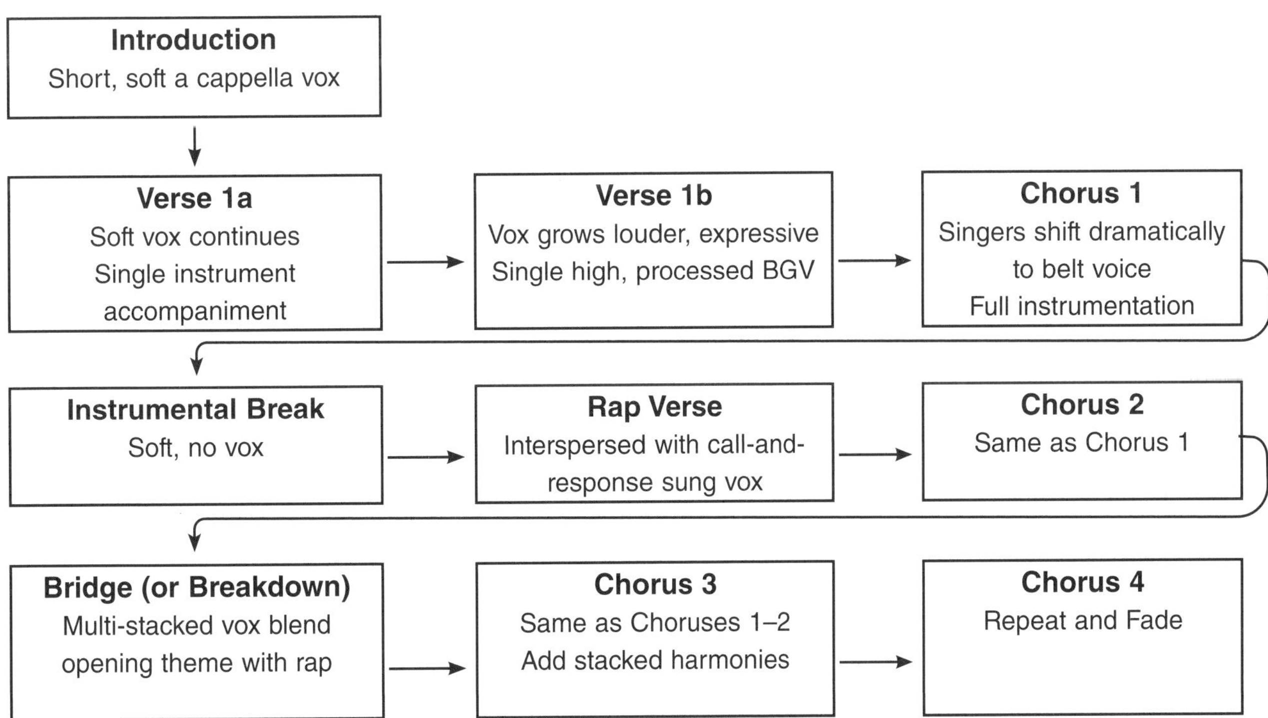

FIG. 2.2. Storyboard Example for a Pop Song with a Rap Feature

LEAD VOCAL ARRANGING

Lead vocals can be arranged in various ways depending on the genre. The least complicated way is for one vocalist to sing the song, without any additional vocal parts. The arrangement of this vocal performance can take advantage of certain accentuators, such as moans, groans, vocal fry (see page 23), and cries. For example, reference "Someone You Loved" by Lewis Capaldi (2018), or the grunts and breaths that were integral to Michael Jackson's style, such as on "Billie Jean" (1983).

If you are in a genre that references strongly back to the blues, such as R&B or rock, for example, accentuators are going to be important for the vocal performance. Other genres may minimize accentuators in favor of a cleaner vocal approach, such as "Haven't Met You Yet" by Michael Bublé (2009) or "Breathe" by Faith Hill (1999).

Other important arrangement considerations are dynamics, pauses or rests, short tones, long tones, use of articulation, use of space, vibrato, bending notes, straight onset of notes, and so on. (Refer to chapter 4 for an in-depth discussion of vocal techniques you can use in your productions.)

While it may not seem like these nuances are part of lead vocal arranging, they can transform a simple performance into something compelling.

DOUBLING AND TRIPLING

If you want to add more voices to your song, the lead vocalist is no longer a single voice in the song. Unison doubles or triples can be used as another kind of accentuator. When doubling, certain words or passages are recorded separately from the lead vocal in unison, which fattens up the lead. Doubling usually places both vocals in the center of the stereo field. This technique can be used to end phrases, emphasize phrases, or make hook moments in the chorus pop out, and so on. Tripling is used similarly to accentuate a lead vocal, but the second and third vocal are typically placed to the left and the right, while the lead vocals remains in the center of the stereo field. (See chapter 5.) One example of a unison triple is the chorus of "Wrecking Ball" by Miley Cyrus (2013).

ADDING HARMONIES

Mapping out the lead vocal helps you to decide where harmonies might be complimentary. Harmony is when two or more notes of different pitches are performed at the same time. It is one of the three main aspects of music along with melody and rhythm. Learning how to harmonize is a skill that may have been picked up naturally at home singing around the piano, singing in the car with the radio, while listening to recordings, singing with friends at school, or singing with others in worship or in a chorus. Most musical genres utilize harmonies. A cappella groups (singing without instrumentation), gospel groups, and choirs always employ harmony.

To harmonize well, vocalists must blend their voices with other singer(s) without standing out, while performing notes that support the melody within the harmonic structure of that point in the song. Well-executed harmonies also have matched vowels, diction, pronunciation (such as a regional accent), rhythmic accuracy, and dynamics. Being aware of the strengths and weaknesses of your vocalists' harmonic chops can make or break your song.

How do you find your note when harmonizing? Experienced singers, learning parts that were already recorded, commonly work out who is going to sing which part in rehearsal. They practice their parts with the recording, with a keyboard, and together a cappella to work on blend and diction. When arranging new parts, each vocalist needs to hear harmonic tones in the supporting chords.

For many genres, vocal harmonies draw from the notes within a given chord: the first note, the third note, and the fifth note of a major scale create the major chord triad (Do, Mi, Sol). A minor harmony would be the first note, the flatted (or minor) third note, and the fifth note of a minor scale chord (Do, Me, Sol). These notes can be stacked in any order depending on the vocal arrangement. For instance, instead of 1-3-5 of the scale, it could be 3-5-1 of the scale, or 5-1-3 of the scale.

The examples in figure 2.3 are in the key of C, but of course there are twelve major and minor keys that harmonies can be applied to. Jazz harmonies are usually more complex, using more than just these three primary notes. The audio tracks illustrate major vs. minor. Each track has a C major scale, C natural minor scale, C major chord arpeggio, and C minor chord arpeggio, with track 2 performing them on a keyboard and track 3 using voice.

2, 3

a.

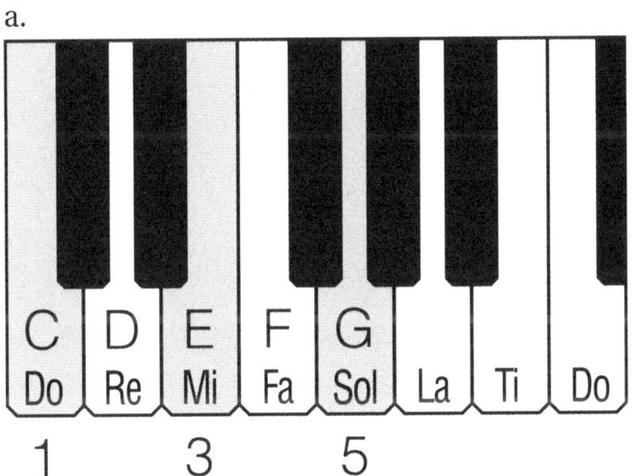

b.

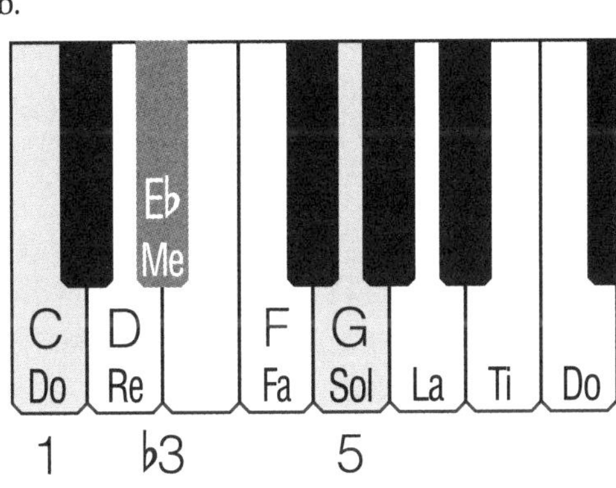

FIG. 2.3. Keyboard Triads. (a) C Major Triad: 1, 3, 5, (b) C Minor Triad: 1, ♭3, 5

Another consideration is whether a harmony part should be sung above or below the melody. This is determined by aesthetic decisions and by the vocal quality of the singers. When the lead vocalist sings their own backing parts, sometimes they need to sound different in timbre from the lead, so that the lead retains focus during the performance. Techniques that achieve a timbral difference include things like singing with a breathier tone, using a different register (chest, head, mix), a nasal sound, etc.

Some examples of recording artists who are geniuses at arranging vocals are Freddy Mercury of Queen; Brian Wilson of the Beach Boys; Ashford and Simpson; Destiny's Child; the Beatles; the Staple Singers; the Everly Brothers; the Platters; the Shirelles; Simon and Garfunkel; the Eagles; Boyz to Men; Earth, Wind, and Fire; Peter, Paul, and Mary; and Crosby, Stills, Nash, and Young. Solo artists such as Elvis Presley, Joni Mitchell, Laura Nyro, Van Morrison, Dan and Shay, Kacey Musgraves, and Bruno Mars use harmonies extensively in their arrangements.

There are many different ways to harmonize. Harmony can be a duet, with tight vocals that match the lead vocal with precision, or thick, unison stacks that fatten up the lead vocal.

Duets

A *duet* is when two people make music together, whether vocalists or instrumentalists. Two voices may blend seamlessly so that you can't tell who's who, such as siblings Nick and Joe Jonas. Or, they may sound very different from one another, like the smooth voice of Alison Krauss and the rough voice of Robert Plant on their collaboration album *Raising Sand* (2007).

Typically, in a duet one person takes the melody while the other sings the harmony, choosing a note either above or below the melody line that fits with the chord changes.

Marvin Gaye and Tammi Terrell, in their classic song "Ain't No Mountain High Enough" (1970) by Ashford and Simpson, give us a romantic and inspirational duet during the Motown era. In the number 1 hit "More Than Words" by Extreme (1989), Gary Cherone's and Nuno Bettencourt's voices blend well, while still maintaining their separate musical personalities. In the duet "Gangnam Station Gate 4" by the K-pop group Plastic (2015) featuring Sean Lee, multiple stacked harmonies and doubled melodic lines fatten up the sound. Lady Gaga and actor Bradley Cooper created a powerhouse duet with the song "Shallow" from the movie remake, *A Star is Born* (2018). The iconic jazz singer Tony Bennett recorded several duet albums performing the classics with other celebrities from non-jazz musical genres.

Background Vocals

A group of background vocalists (BGVs) is usually made up of two to three people who support a song by doubling or harmonizing with the lead vocal, singing a part that weaves around the lead vocal, and/or filling out the chorus and hook lines with harmonies. (A "hook" is a repeated phrase in a song that is catchy and memorable.)

Sometimes, the artist will sing all the backgrounds in a recording, such as multiple stacked parts by Freddy Mercury of the band Queen. When the lead singer who recorded their own background parts performs in concert, a group of singers may be added to the live ensemble in order to sing the parts, and/or harmony samples from the original recording can be triggered by computer. It is common to see background singers on stage behind any number of famous artists and bands, moving together as a unit, and adding an additional element for the audience to watch and listen to, even though the recorded vocals may have been sung by one person. The movie *Twenty Feet from Stardom* (2013) offers a deep look into the life of several top-tier professional background singers and how they work both in and out of the studio.

BGV harmonies can also complement the lead vocal without trying to match it, filling out the harmony of a chord by singing "ooh's" under the lead, as in the song "It's So Hard to Say Goodbye" by the group Boyz II Men (1991). Or, the harmonies can function like a wall of sound emulating a synthesizer, as in "Wonder" by Shawn Mendes (2020) that recorded a multi-stacked, five-person choir.

By matching the lead vocal performance precisely in diction, timing, dynamics, and articulation, well-synchronized BGVs add density and fullness to a recording. The singers might choose notes to flesh out a chord, double the lead vocal in unison (or in octaves), or both. This way of harmonizing is precise, sometimes resulting in a blending of voices for which it is hard to distinguish one singer from another. One singer may also record all the parts individually to achieve this effect.

Synchronized singers breathe together and match their movements to aid in their precision. Sometimes, the harmonies are recorded first after the *scratch vocal* sets up the song; then the lead vocalist comes back in to lay down the final performance and fit with the harmonies. (A scratch vocal is an informal recording, used as a reference for the instrumentalists and producer. In some cases, if it's a really good performance, the scratch vocal is kept as the final vocal.)

Some examples of synchronized singing are "Lying Eyes" by the Eagles (1975) and "Bang Bang" by Jesse J, Ariana Grande, and Nicki Minaj (2014). Each one of these groupings can add one or more additional harmony notes, placed in the mix in the same manner. Two notable songs with stacks panned on the left, right, and center are "I Look to You" by Whitney Houston (2009), and "Little Freak" by Harry Styles (2022).

Most vocal producers record no more than two voices per panning position within the stereo field (left, center, and right). This is because if you record more than two identical unison tracks and pan them to the same panning position, the lyrics can become harder to understand, and a slight effect called *comb filtering* can result. True comb-filtering occurs when a vocal part is copied, pasted, placed in the same panning position, and shifted a small amount (1 to 7 milliseconds) away. This makes the vocals sound metallic. So, when you want to add more than two voices and use the same panning position for the additional voices, it's helpful to change the timbre of those additional voices. Using a different vocal quality in unison on the same note will always minimize any potential for comb filtering.

Sometimes, harmonies coordinate with the lead vocal but don't match it exactly. Loosely synchronized harmonies are common in improvisational styles such as gospel, R&B, and country, as in the song "Suite: Judy Blue Eyes" by Crosby, Stills, and Nash (1969). Another example of synchronized harmonies that are under a loose lead vocal is the song "All About That Bass" by Meghan Trainor (2014).

In songs where the harmonies either carry the hook line or provide an answer to the lead singer (call-and-response), they serve to anchor the song while providing space for the lead singer to sing freely on top. Some examples of a loose lead vocal against supportive background harmonies are "Respect," performed by Aretha Franklin (1965), "Ain't Nobody," by Chaka Khan (1983), "Confessions Part II" by Usher (2004) and "positions" by Ariana Grande (2020).

Background vocals are so commonplace that you may not even realize you are hearing them. They can be placed far back in the mix to create a "pad"-like instrumental quality and to fill out the tapestry of the recording. Or they can be prominent in a song and iconic to its sound, as in groups like the Andrews Sisters from the 1930s, '40s, and '50s that feature several singers in the lead position. Groups that typically sing in harmony include the Chicks (previously known as the Dixie Chicks), NSYNC, the Band Perry, New Edition, and the Spice Girls—notably their song "Wannabe" (2020).

In the following classic songs with background vocals, individual backgrounds can have a more prominent focus in the song, for example: "You Can't Hurry Love" by the Supremes (1966), with Diana Ross on most of the lead vocals, and backgrounds provided by Florence Ballard and Mary Wilson; "Help Me" by Joni Mitchell (1974), all parts sung by Joni Mitchell; "I Want It That Way" by the Back Street Boys (1999); and "Victoria's Secret" by Jax (2022).

Choirs

While it's likely that you have an idea what a choir (or chorus) is, let's define it within the context of tracking a large vocal group for your song. A typical choir is a group of vocalists organized by their vocal type, SATB: soprano (traditionally higher female range up to C6 or D6), alto (traditionally lower female range from F3 to E5), tenor (traditionally higher male range from C3 to G4), and bass (traditionally lowest male range, no lower than E3). Choir groups can be any size and formation, and are found all around the world in schools, houses of worship, on stage, and in local venues. Several voices sing in unison on a part within their vocal type, and together the parts blend to create harmony, either accompanied by instruments, or singing a cappella.

As with an orchestra, a choir has a musical director who makes sure individual voices blend well together and are balanced between the parts. The director pays attention to the musical shape of each piece, including dynamics, timing, the use of space (rests and phrasing), places to breathe, vowel shape, and where to place the ending consonants of words. Sometimes, the director has to ask people from different regions to adjust their natural speaking accent so the timbre of their vowels match. That is in part because the shape of a vowel—which is contoured within the mouth and throat—affects both intonation and the harmonic balance of a note. Moving where people are standing in the group can also correct inconsistencies in tone. Depending on the style of music they are performing, choirs may also move together with gestures and steps. (See chapter 6 for more about best recording practices in reverberant spaces.)

Popular songs often incorporate choral singing into their arrangements. For example, in the song "drivers license" by Olivia Rodrigo (2021), the second half of the song features a full choir. For this purpose, a choir might be recorded in a produced session, using several different takes of the same parts, to fatten out the sound. Another example is the iconic pop song "We Are the World" (1985), for which several celebrity singers came together as a choir in a rare group moment to record Michael Jackson's and Lionel Ritchie's song to raise money for famine in Africa. In order to align several takes of the group, the choir director would have been listening to the band and possibly a click track.

While you can record a group of people with one microphone, a standard engineering practice for recording a choir is to use two or more microphones for a wide image within the stereo field. Think of the choir as one large instrument similar to a synthesizer pad, and with individual vocal timbres. For solo phrases that need more focus, the soloist may have a handheld mic, or come up to a mic on a stand. In that case, the soloist's part could be recorded on a separate track from the group.

DOUBLE-TRACKING AND WHISPER TRACKS

The sung vocals on a recording can be augmented by techniques such as double-tracking, whispering, and spoken vocals. These can be added to a song in any number of ways to create an arrangement that adds texture, tone, and dynamic variations.

Double-tracking is when the vocalist doubles their lead vocal, and both takes are heard in the mix. This technique fattens up the lead vocal performance. The goal is to sing the double identically to the original vocal. Since no person can perform a precise copy of the original vocal, the end result is a chorus effect, as in the bridge section (2:10) of "Firework" by Katy Perry (2010), where both takes are panned center. You can also use this technique for recording BGVs. The double can be placed at the same volume level as the main vocal, or at a softer level. Your choice of volume levels for the double can affect the emotional connection to both the lyric and the listener.

A *whisper track* doubles the vocal with a spoken whisper. In the video (currently on YouTube) *The Doors - Riders On The Storm (Jim Morrison's Whisper Vocal Rain Percussion, Very Rare) (1971)*, you can hear Jim Morrison's whisper track soloed. Whispering can add a ghostly effect to the lead vocal performance, and is used in many popular recordings so subtly, that it can be difficult to hear. To create a whisper track, record the vocalist at close proximity to the microphone (be sure to use a pop filter), whispering the song along with the previously recorded lead vocal. Modern producers also use saturation plug-ins to create an artificial sound that mimics whispering. Take a listen to Halsey's saturated vocal in "Without Me" (2020) that has a ghostly air in every line of her performance.

CHAPTER 3

Vocal Coaching

There is perhaps nothing more intimate than recording the human voice. Anytime a voice is recorded, it becomes an indelible expression of the artist, and who they are in that time of their life. This recording will last for years to come. You want the vocal to sound amazing—the best it can be performed.

When you are the producer, your role is part artistic director and part vocal coach. A skilled coach provides feedback to help the vocalist achieve their sound, while offering objectivity about their performance. In return, the vocalist needs to trust you completely in this role. Therefore, establishing a solid and safe working environment is essential for a successful project.

Your primary focus when recording is on the *product*: the song, the quality of the recording, and staying in line with the commercial objectives of the project. This is often different from what is needed in a live performance, because what works on stage may not be right for the sonic spectrum of the recording. So, a vocalist who is accustomed mainly to live performing will find recording to be a different experience. That's because unlike in a live setting, where vocals are usually performed with no or minimal corrections, a recorded vocal can be corrected, adjusted, and modified. Therefore, what you hear in a finished recording is often not what the vocalist sounded like live in the room. The voice of a known artist you have come to love may also *not* sound the same if you could hear them unprocessed.

In addition, if you're self-producing, staying objective may be harder than when you have a second pair of ears to offer feedback. It also takes time to become familiar with how your recorded voice sounds, compared with how it sounds in a live space. This is because hearing your voice vibrating inside your head sounds different from the tonal color of your voice captured by a microphone within a recording. As you record, you may even be hearing both your natural voice in your head as well as the recorded vocal. For these reasons, feedback from a skilled vocal coach may be helpful.

In the past, a vocal producer—even against the wishes of a vocal coach—might have had a singer working for several hours with minimal breaks. That kind of rigor can push the vocalist to the point of blowing out their voice. That is death to the voice, even potentially causing permanent damage. With today's technology, the endless number of tracks that are available in a DAW could encourage doing take after take until you get the result you want, with the same risk of vocal damage.

However, when today's technology is used well, fewer takes may be needed to get a solid vocal performance. A shorter session is possible because an efficient producer listens to the vocalist while also calculating how the production tools—such as Auto-Tune, equalizers, reverb, etc.—will service the performance after the vocalist leaves. Always keep in mind that the maximum amount of time a vocalist should sing without risking vocal fatigue or even injury is about two or three hours, with periodic short breaks, especially for techniques that can stress the voice.

In many genres (particularly popular styles), the recording process has evolved to be something like airbrushing the voice, modifying the recording with engineering techniques in order to produce the best overall song. It's like making a film with edits, cuts, and digital processing. The exceptions to vocal processing would be in genres like jazz and folk music, in which the recording is of an uninterrupted performance.

EFFECTIVE COACHING AND FEEDBACK

Our voices are personal. They are a part of us—part of our identity, and just like faces, no two voices are exactly the same. The human voice is an expression of the soul. Using the voice expressively with emotion may make the vocalist feel vulnerable. Feeling insecure or unsure about how they sound is normal. When the recording button is pushed, it is common for a vocalist to have one of these worries: "What if my song doesn't come out well?" "What if my voice cracks?" "What if all the fancy tricks in the world just can't make my voice sound great?" "What if the final vocal just doesn't even sound like *me*?"

Creating a trusting relationship with the vocalist from the beginning is important to help ease these anxieties. The vocalist needs to be comfortable with you as a producer, or recordist, and accept your guidance. And, that guidance must be knowledgeable, including how to maintain vocal health throughout the recording process, as well as bringing out the best of that individual's vocal quality.

If the vocalist works with a skilled coach ahead of a recording session, to be well prepared for the rigor of the recording process, keep in mind that there are different ways to coach. A vocal instructor may focus on style, aspects of technique, diction, phrasing, emotional expression, and mic technique, while a producer-as-coach may work on tonal choices, syncopation, performance, and style. Unfortunately, anyone involved in the project who offers vocal advice—A&R executive, management, assistant engineer, Aunt Bessie—is effectively coaching. All coaches, even those not part of the Magic Triangle, should be aware of healthy vocal practices and productive feedback.

YOUR AUTHENTIC VOICE

Imagine being asked to make your voice sound like someone else. Can you make your face look like someone else's? While some vocalists may be able to channel an artist's style to create a vibe, their voice will not sound just like that artist's. This kind of coaching can be destructive in a session and should be avoided.

A vocal coach/instructor may have an opinion about what sounds great and what doesn't; ideally, this guidance won't conflict with the producer's vision. That coach instead offers feedback before and/or during the recording, serves as a cheerleader, a mentor, and a physical coach similar to sports, helping the vocalist prepare artistically, technically, musically, and mentally—and even spiritually. They work on technical aspects including diction, articulation, projection, when to use commonly identified registers (e.g., chest, head, mix, falsetto), posture and alignment, and song interpretation.

The vocal producer is concerned with how the voice sounds in the song, and is actively engaged in the song's specific outcome. The voice can become like a paintbrush within an artificial canvas, the performance painting an aural picture that takes the song to a whole new level.

The vocal recordist working with the producer may comment on whether a take has the right levels, is in tune, conveys impactful emotion, etc. They should be aware of interacting constructively with the producer, keeping the larger project goals in mind, and avoiding too many voices providing feedback for the vocalist.

BEST PRACTICES FOR A HEALTHY VOICE

The vocalist's *entire body* is involved in singing, including posture, energy level, overall physical health, diet, and their vocal habits. The vocalist wants to sound amazing! When investing a great deal of mental and emotional energy into a project—which is necessary to excel—there may also be tension that arises from expecting a great deal from oneself. Tension in turn affects the voice negatively. Thoughts, emotions and expectations have a significant effect on the singing voice. A vocalist may push themselves hard physically to get the recording they want, while beating themselves up mentally if they feel they're not meeting the sound they're going for. Being pushed throughout long hours of a session will lead to vocal and mental exhaustion.

A voice can stay healthy and productive throughout life when well cared for. Think big picture—long past the recording session. The vocalist should be consistent with their healthy habits. This is because once the voice is damaged, it is difficult, if not impossible, to bring it back to health and function. (And you can't buy a replacement voice at the music store.)

It's important for you to know when the vocalist should rest, and when it is okay for them to continue. Listen to them, and encourage them to care for their voice like the irreplaceable instrument that it is. Training to record a song is not anything like training to run a race: leg muscles are big and strong, but vocal muscles are tiny, and easily strained. They cannot and should not be pushed to the point of fatigue. Instead, encourage the vocalist to pace themselves and take breaks. Also know that if you become demanding, for some, this is inspiring; for others, it causes anxiety, which makes their singing worsen. So, learn each individual person's needs.

Even one incident from pushing the voice into straining can damage it permanently.

Do's and Don'ts

While each voice is different, there are common do's and don'ts that apply to everyone. How each person uses their voice will vary, even when singing the same song in the same key. Some people can sing for long periods of time without experiencing vocal fatigue or hoarseness, while other voices tire out more easily. Some people can sing a very high note, while others cannot. Some singers can belt out a song easily, while others find that difficult. If you're not sure whether the vocalist is working too hard or whether they're truly doing fine, *ask them!* And if self-producing, be honest with yourself. Learn to recognize the signs of vocal exhaustion and fatigue, such as if their voice gives out, their tone changes, or their high notes are now harder to sing.

Warming up the voice well before a session and during practice is important. Too often, vocalists think they can warm up their voices for five or ten minutes then jump right into a song. This is bad for a number of reasons. First, the tissues and muscles within the voice need to be actually *warm* in order to be flexible. A cold voice will not respond well, and can be injured more readily, especially when a singing technique is physically demanding, such as belting (high, powerful singing). Second, if the vocalist hasn't practiced the song, how can they sing it well? Could a dancer perform a routine they've never learned? Can an athlete excel on the field without training regularly? Obviously, no. How much warmup and practice should be done before recording depends on how demanding the song is, as well as each vocalist's specific vocal body and routine. Challenging music requires flexibility exercises for finer motor vocal control, needing even more prep time.

Maintaining vocal health in the studio is essential, where long hours, poor food, and late nights are often a part of recording. It is important to support the vocalist's self-care, including sticking to a list of healthy do's and don'ts.

Here are some session practices that are generally healthy and unhealthy for the vocalist. Be sure the vocalists are well-hydrated before you start the session.

Healthy Session Practices	Unhealthy Session Practices
Warming up adequately before getting to songs, so the voice feels supple and flexible. Thirty minutes is best, starting out gently.	Starting the warmup too aggressively and jumping right into harder exercises or songs, or pushing the voice hard to the point of vocal fatigue or hoarseness.
Gargling with warm salt water for an irritated throat, phlegm, or allergies.	Clearing one's throat loudly, such as "hocking" to remove mucus. This causes the vocal folds to slam together. It is hard on the voice (and it's gross!).
Practicing low, slow, supported breathing, while maintaining good, balanced posture.	Breathing upwards toward the shoulders or high in the rib cage. Slouching.
Speaking at a neutral volume with conscious breath support.	Speaking loudly, such as trying to be heard over a loud playback. Yelling or screaming, speaking in "fry" voice, or whispering for long periods.
Massaging the jaw, face, and temples.	Craning the neck, reaching up to the mic. Straining up for "high notes."
Drinking room temperature beverages throughout the session that hydrate, including room temperature or warm water, herbal tea, and natural juices. Carbonated water is okay, though causes burping.	Drinking a lot of caffeinated beverages, especially without adequate water intake. Eating foods that cause mucus (typically, dairy products, spicy foods, etc.).
Resting the voice during the session as needed.	Singing in any manner that gets a desired outcome, regardless of the consequences.
Clear, circulating air in the studio.	Smoking or vaping—anything. That goes for second-hand smoke, too.
Gentle, clear, lower-to-mid pitched vocalizations to help when the voice is irritated, or vocal rest.	Singing when sick or having a sore throat, which leads to compensating for swollen or irritated vocal folds, making singing worse.

Here are some lifestyle practices that are impactful for the vocalist to maintain for an optimal voice. This includes how they speak, too; it's the same instrument whether speaking or singing.

Healthy Lifestyle Practices	Unhealthy Lifestyle Practices
Staying well-hydrated throughout the day, ideally with room-temperature water, to maintain healthy vocal folds.	Not drinking enough water throughout the day, which dehydrates the body, and in turn dries out the voice.
Steaming the voice, either in the shower, over a pot of hot water with a towel, or with a purchased face steamer. Or, using a nasal rinse with distilled water and saline solution.	Taking medicines that dry out the throat, such as decongestants and some antihistamines. Use these with discretion when needed.
Keeping the voice in shape—daily, including regular vocalizing.	Smoking or vaping—anything. That goes for second-hand smoke, too.
Eating no closer than two to three hours before bedtime, to avoid stomach acid rising into the throat.	Eating foods and beverages that cause acid reflux (GERD), which will irritate the voice.

AIR FLOW: BREATHING AND BREATH SUPPORT

It all begins with breathing. Most people think they suck in air to breathe, because it feels that way. In fact, the most important function of the larynx, where the vocal folds are located, is breathing! The first thing that actually happens—which is important for the vocalist to understand—is movement of the diaphragm, the primary muscle for breathing. Located in the middle of the torso, it separates the heart and lungs from the digestive organs.

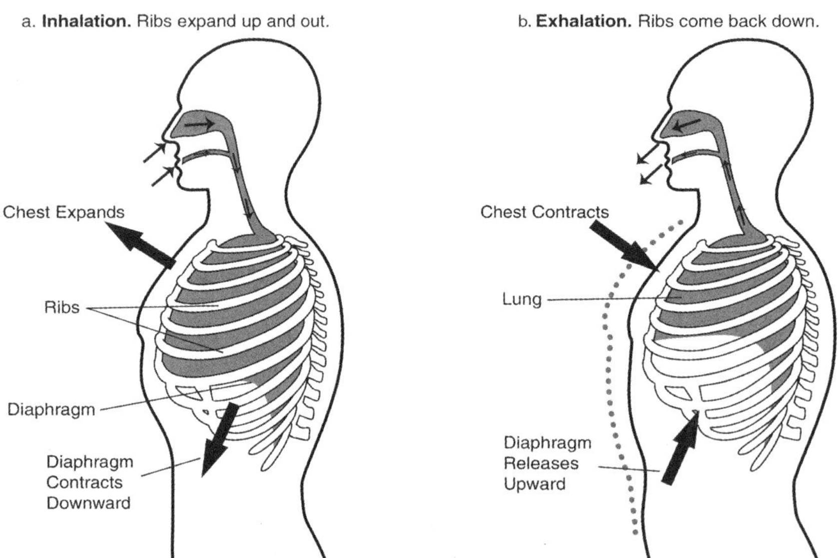

FIG. 3.1. Process of (a) Inhalation (b) Exhalation

- *Inhalation* (breathing in) happens when the diaphragm first contracts downward as the ribs expand outward and slightly up, which in turn creates space in the chest cavity, and thus a decrease in air pressure. This decrease in air pressure creates a vacuum that sucks air into the lungs to fill them.
- During *exhalation* (breathing out), the diaphragm muscle relaxes upwards while the ribs come back inward and down. This pushes air

back out from the lungs, past the vocal folds, and out through the nose and/or mouth.

(For this reason, if someone coaches the vocalist to "breathe from the diaphragm," they are offering confusing instructions, because that is physiologically impossible.) Breath support is the slow release of that air pressure, which is needed to activate the vocal folds, similar to holding the breath and releasing it gradually. When we speak, we tend to inhale at the last minute before saying something, even squeezing out words at the end of a sentence. This does not work well for singing or speaking. Experienced vocalists know to maintain a feeling of comfortable fullness of air in their lungs *before* they sing, then regulate the release of air as they produce sound. They do this by engaging their core abdominal and rib muscles, inhaling sooner and more slowly, while keeping their neck free and chin relaxed. This is called "breath support," "breath management," or "breath control."

15 MINUTE BREATHING CONTROL EXERCISES

Track 4 provides a set of "15 Minute Breathing Control Exercises." These are:

4

1. Breath Exercise: Ah Ah Ah Ah Ah, Hold. Repeat five times.
2. Breath Exercise Countdown
3. 1-3-1 Glide
4. 1-5-1 Glide
5. Holding a Note
6. Ma May Mi Mo Mu
7. Octave Glide
8. Ya: 5-4-3-2-1
9. Oo Ee: 1-2-3-4-5-4-3-2 (two times), then 1-2-3-4-5-6-7-8-9-8-7-6-5-4-3-2-1

VOCAL TYPES, RANGES, AND REGISTERS

The classical definition of vocal types is generally bass, baritone, tenor, alto, mezzo soprano, and soprano. In Western traditional literature, knowing one's vocal type is important; however, it is less so for popular contemporary styles, where the focus is on the individual quality of the vocalist's sound. For example, the artist Drake is a baritone, Ed Sheeran is a tenor, Beyoncé is an alto, and Ariana Grande is a soprano.

A *vocal range* is defined as the highest and lowest notes one can sing *comfortably*, even though they may have audible pitches above or below that range. While it is possible to be born with a large range, or to expand it through training, for the average person, each vocal type has roughly a two-octave range, the quality of which is characterized by the register they are using. Understanding where their voice is the most comfortable also corresponds to where their vocal quality is usually the most resonant and reliable. Tracks 5 to 10 demonstrate commonly accepted vocal ranges for the various voice types. You can use the acronym F A C to determine generally defined ranges, referring to the pitches F, A, and C:

5–10

C3–C5: Tenor	C4–C6: Soprano
A2–A4: Baritone	A3–A5: Mezzo Soprano
F2–F4: Bass	F3–F5: Alto

A *vocal register* is an area of the voice that has a definable quality to it, produced by specific muscles in the larynx (voice box) that generate the voice. Most people have three or four definable vocal registers within their overall vocal range, and these can overlap. Note that these definitions change depending on whom you're asking, and as vocal research unfolds new understanding. The most recent voice research informs us that there are actually just two registers: Mode 1 and Mode 2, each with a complex set of muscular movements that are distinct from one another in how they sound and in how they function. These movements generate the other definable registers and non-register techniques.

Vocal tones are generated by the tiny vocal folds, which vibrate together at the same frequency as any instrument on the same pitch. The vocal folds shorten and fatten to producer lower notes, and can loosen tension on the voice. The vocal folds stretch longer and thinner for higher notes. Tenors and basses often have slightly larger vocal folds than altos and sopranos, about the proportions of a nickel to a dime.

While there is not one standard definition of vocal registers, these description are generally accepted, and many singers with formal educations will likely be aware of them.

low voice

11–16

Also called *chest voice* or *mode 1*. It can produce a soft sound with low air pressure or a strong, stout sound, requiring more air pressure. The *speaking voice*, also called the *modal register*, resides in mode 1 for most people. When staying in chest voice while ascending in pitch, straining may occur if the vocalist doesn't know how to make adjustments to lessen air pressure. Tenors and basses will usually stay in chest voice until reaching their *passaggio* (the area of transition between registers, as follows). For most, this is in the area of C4 (middle C, 261.62 Hz) to A4, where the switch occurs into falsetto or head voice. This switch is usually easier for tenors than for most baritones or basses. Altos may use chest voice more than sopranos, beginning around F3 and potentially pushing up to B4 at the highest. High sopranos may not have the anatomy to produce a strong chest voice.

high voice

17–22

Also called *head voice* for altos and sopranos, and *falsetto* for tenors and basses, and *mode 2*. In popular commercial styles, falsetto and head voice are very common. Head voice in tenors and basses is actually a blending of modes 1 and 2, not pure falsetto. Occasionally, however, you may hear head voice referred to as falsetto, even though they are different anatomically. In most Western classical singing, basses and tenors are not trained to use their falsetto. Examples of artists who use both head voice and falsetto are Justin Timberlake and Bruno Mars in pop, Kenny Rankin in jazz, Steven Tyler of Aerosmith, and Steven Perry of Journey in rock. An interesting example of singing exclusively in falsetto is Robin Thicke's performance on "Lost Without U" (2006). For most sopranos, especially younger vocalists, singing in head voice is the most comfortable, and the most commonly recorded. Their head voice range is wide: approximately from E4 to G5 and above; notes in the fourth octave (C4 to B4) are often breathy or hard to produce in mode 2. You may notice a big change in tone between their chest and head voices. Examples of head voice performances are "When You Say Nothing at All" by Alison Krauss (1999) and the chorus of "Both Sides Now" by Joni Mitchell (1966), which hit #8 in the Top 100s when covered by Judy Collins in 1967.

mix voice Occurs as the muscles of modes 1 and 2 work together. The term also references a tonal quality that is used in many genres such as musical theater, country, and R&B. It is bright, forward, and sometimes *twangy* sounding, meaning somewhat nasal. It enables strong tones while being less strenuous on the voice than full chest voice. Head voice in a tenor or bass is an example of mixing, such as Russell Thompkins Jr.'s performance in "People Make the World Go Round" by the Stylistics (1971). Both altos and sopranos tend to sing in a lighter mix voice for their middle range, around C4 to C5, then switch to head voice for upper notes beginning around B4 to E5. Mix voice can be used alongside other registers to create variations within a performance. An example is the opening verse of "Glitter in the Air" by P!NK (2008).

23–24

whistle tone A rarer soprano register that reaches extremely high notes, even A6 or B6! It is produced by a different use of the vocal muscles, and most people aren't able to produce it. Whistle tone is performed by artists such as Ariana Grande, Minnie Riperton ("Loving You," 1975) and Mariah Carey. James Brown's E♭6 in "The Payback" (1973) may be an unusual example of tenor whistle tone.

passaggio Also called *transition*, it is a region in between registers, usually about an interval of a fourth. In the passaggio, the laryngeal muscles are shifting in between modes 1 and 2, which makes singing more complex, and usually feels awkward to navigate. An example is the when a tenor or bass switches between their full voice and falsetto. Sometimes, this region is called a "break." Listen to track 25's examples of a soprano singer in passaggio:

- in between her chest voice (mode 1) and mix voice, and
- in between her mix voice and head voice (mode 2).

25

NON-REGISTER TECHNIQUES

While you may hear the following techniques referred to as registers in production terminology, they are in fact non-register techniques and can be effective to achieve a desired style or tone when working in contemporary popular genres.

belting Sometimes confused as a register—as in the misleading instruction, "sing in your belt register"—belting is a *quality* of singing that is loud, passionate, and dramatic. Belting can be produced with (1) mode 1 (chest voice), (2) strong mix voice, and/or (3) mode 1 and mix voice. Belting is often most effective when interspersed within a phrase or song, rather than on every note (which is also vocally exhausting). Examples of mix voice belting can be heard in most songs performed by Jesse J, and in Olivia Rodrigo's #1 hit song "drivers license" (2021). Examples of belting using only mode 1 are songs by Adele, and rock singer Joe Cocker—in both cases leading to vocal damage, unfortunately. Although there are individuals who can belt in mode 1 without harming their voices, for most people if pushed too hard or straining, consistent belting can cause vocal damage. (To learn more about belting, please see Jeannie Gagné's book *Belting:*

A Guide to Powerful, Healthy Singing, from Berklee Press).

fry voice Defined by a loose vibration of the vocal folds, in or below the speaking range. It sounds like the person just woke up or has a sore throat, and has become a ubiquitous quality of speaking. While fry voice may be effective to create an intimate vocal effect, continuous use of fry voice—whether singing or speaking—causes the vocal muscles to be lazy and makes other kinds of vocalizing more difficult. In fact, pushing out sound through a scratchy speaking voice—which is such a common speaking style these days—can easily lead to vocal problems. One example of fry voice is in the verses of Britney Spears' #1 hit song, "Womanizer" (2008).

glottal stop (pop) A sound that happens when there is a burst of air at the start of a note that causes the vocal folds to slam together. It is a moment in a vocalization, not a register, though may be referred to as one. The harsh nature of glottal stops cause unhealthy impacts to the voice, and with repeated use will likely result in vocal swelling, and even damage, such as nodules. This impact increases with higher notes. Sometimes, singers use a glottal stop effect lower in their range, making the phrasing sound more speechlike. Sam Smith uses a glottal stop frequently during the song "I'm Not the Only One" (2014), especially in the bridge. Use this effect sparingly. If the vocalist is tiring easily, it is possible they are beginning or ending their phrases habitually with a glottal stop. Point out the sound they are making to help them to adjust away from this pattern.

yodeling An effect used in many cultures worldwide, and can be heard commonly in American country music dating back generations. It occurs when the note begins on a strong lower pitch, then flips quickly up onto a higher, lighter note. A fun example of yodeling is "The Lonely Goatherd" from the musical *The Sound of Music* (1965).

As you can see, it's important for the producer to understand how a vocalist uses their voice to avoid confusing them while guiding them to the result you want, and because these effects can harm the voice if not produced in a healthy way. A useful approach is to use words that you and the vocalist both understand when referring to any of these techniques.

Tone

The tone of each person's voice is unique to them, determined by the resonant spaces within the anatomical structures of their vocal tract. Their sound is influenced by how they speak, their native language, whether they're a loud or soft talker, and—significantly—their ideas about what good singing sounds like. When seeking a specific quality of sound from the vocalist, consider: Is their natural tone clean, breathy, or scratchy? Is it nasal or clear? Warm or bright? Placed forward in the mouth or in the back? Deep and full sounding or high and light? A skilled vocalist knows how to adjust their voice to create these different tonal characteristics. Let's take a deeper look at how these different sounds are produced.

A *clean tone* has little air in the sound and is not nasal. This is the *bel canto* voice of Western traditional singing. A clean tone is accomplished by (1) full closure of the vocal folds so minimal air "leaks" there, and (2) lifting the *soft palate* in the back of the throat, which closes off the airway to the sinuses while making ample space in the areas of the mouth and throat to amplify sound. Chest-belt singing also has a clean tone because of the full closure of the folds pressed tightly together.

A *breathy tone* is produced when the vocal folds are apart somewhat while phonating, allowing some air to be heard in the sound. While a breathy tone is used to create intimacy in a performance, be aware that the vocalist will have less air to work with and may need to sing shorter phrases.

A *nasal tone* comes from some air escaping through the sinuses, or producing upwards pressure in the mouth. This tone is heard in some styles such as country music (Willie Nelson) and hip-hop (Lil Wayne). A voice will also sound nasal when the sinuses are blocked, such as with a head cold or allergies.

A *warm tone* refers to a sound that has less high frequency resonance than a *bright* tone. Think about the meaning of the song to help determine the tone you want to get. For example, romantic songs might work well with a warm tone, whereas for an upbeat, excited song, you might want the tone to be bright.

26–30

Listen to tracks 26 to 30 for examples of the different voice types singing various tones (26 bass, 27 baritone, 28 tenor, 29 alto, 30 soprano), each singing:

1. a clean tone
2. a breathy tone
3. a nasal tone
4. a bright tone, and
5. a warm tone

31

Track 31 illustrates vocal placement: first forward, then neutral, then back. *Forward placement* means the sound is aimed toward the front of the mouth, which brightens the tone. *Back placement* means the opposite: the sound resonates more in back of the mouth, which makes the tone fuller-sounding, "darker," and warmer. Back placement may also tighten muscles in the back of the throat and tongue, which is a common cause of straining. Therefore, to reduce tension, the vocalist can imagine lengthening their throat while relaxing their tongue.

Timbre refers to the specific harmonic content of the notes that are produced by a vocalist. The harmonic content of each individual varies based upon their anatomy. A vocalist can adjust their harmonic content by how they shape their mouth when producing a specific vowel. Recordists manipulate harmonic content when they EQ a vocal performance. Track 32 illustrates filtering, first with a neutral (unfiltered) phrase, then the phrase filtered forward, then the phrase filtered back, to create different timbres. See chapter 4 for more on timbre.

32

Diction

Words are composed of vowels and consonants. Vowels provide the tone, resonance, and volume of the voice. Consonants provide word clarity, punctuation, and percussive sounds. How words are shaped impacts tone, and whether the voice feels free or tight. Some vowels are more closed naturally than others because of how the mouth shapes them. When singing higher notes, typically, vowels are modified so that they don't sound constricted. For example, the "ee" (as in "me") vowel may be modified to an "eh" sound, and the "oo" vowel (as in "you") may be modified to "oh."

Sharp or Flat?

Words with "ee" vowels tend to sharpen a note, while words with "ah" vowels tend to flatten. If your vocalist is having intonation problems, one reason could be their vowel position. Another reason could be whether they are letting their air support drop (flatting), or pushing out the note too hard (sharpening). Have the vocalist try different shapes in their mouth to adjust their intonation.

SELECTING THE KEY

Unless you're working with a pre-fixed arrangement, the vocalist doesn't need to perform a song in the original key. Look instead for the best key that suits their voice.

- The highest note in the melody should be comfortable for the vocalist, since you don't want them to strain. If the lowest note is too low, choose a key that balances between that and the highest note. Or, consider modifying the melody if necessary to make a lower key work.
- Ideally, the strongest or focal part of the song should sit in the area of the vocalist's range that is most comfortable and free, and not in their passaggio. This is because passaggios are tricky to navigate, and forcing out a melody there can lead to a less than ideal performance, or even straining.
- Can the vocalist deliver the hook or chorus of the song without straining? For prerecorded tracks, the key should fit the vocalist's vocal range and registration. Transpose the key using the DAW, if needed.

PREPARING FOR A RECORDED VOCAL PERFORMANCE

These tips are helpful while preparing for the recording session, both for the vocalist and for the producer who is coaching the vocalist. Vocalists should:

- Practice performing with headphones on, to get accustomed to the sound of their voice without hearing it in the room.
- Memorize how to use the full body for each song. It is normal and important for vocalists to be aware of the whole body as the instrument.
- Practice which vocal register and tone they'll use for each section of a song. Should it be sung breathy or clear? Raspy or smooth? Lower in the overall range or higher? Does the melody move between vocal registers, or does it stay within one?
- Use different ways to shape language within the physical vocal process (mouth, sinuses, and throat). These details are important for the producer to understand.
- Decide what the dynamic range of the song is. Does it contain belting (loud, high, dramatic, passionate singing), for example, or does it stay more mellow and chill?
- Prepare for and practice any difficult notes or passages in the song. Where are those moments?

- Discover if the song is tiring to sing. If so, address technical shifts to remove the fatigue, such as the key, dynamics, and placement, including taking frequent breaks.
- Plan ahead for where breaths occur in between phrases. Is there adequate breath support to get through each phrase?

STYLE PREPARATION

A song's style goes hand in hand with vocal style, and vocal technique. Vocal style includes a wide range of specific details that you need to be aware of. For example, besides the quality of tone, vocal style elements include:

- rhythmic expression
- pronunciation of the lyrics
- using straight tone, or vibrato, or both
- using short, staccato notes, or long, legato notes
- using speech-level technique (singing in the speaking voice and range)
- using dynamics throughout the song
- how intimate or dramatic the performance comes across
- aligning with the song's groove and overall genre

Being familiar with the instrumental track helps a vocalist to perform a song well. It's common for vocalists to focus on the melodic line or the tonal quality of the original singer, but not on the instrumental track in depth. They may miss the nuance of harmonic qualities generated by different synths, guitars, and the like. They may hear the overall sonic tapestry, but not recognize how their vocal fits with it. For example, to help the vocalist hear the rhythmic groove clearly, you can suggest singing along with the bass line. How does the drum groove make them want to move?

Sometimes, there is no instrumentation available for the vocalist to practice with, such as with a new song, or a raw demo that doesn't have much of an arrangement yet. In these situations, typically the instrumental tracks and scratch vocals (see chapter 7) are recorded at the same time. Stem splitting/extraction allows us to isolate vocals and instrumentals from each other. This is a great example of useful Artificial Intelligence (AI). Afterwards, the vocalist can practice with these tracks before coming back to record the final vocal(s).

For the vocalist, working with the full instrumental production can help to get a great vocal take. Performing with headphones on, immersed in the music, can be a transformative experience! The voice sounds different over headphones than it does in an acoustic space. When the producer and recordist hear the same headphone feed as the vocalist, they can advise the vocalist more clearly, as needed.

Unless you're a skilled vocal instructor, don't try to coach singers in vocal technique. That is because coaching someone *how* to sing, when you are not an expert in vocal technique, could be potentially harmful to their voice, or simply confusing. A better strategy is to encourage a calm, yet *active* approach to vocalizing, much like the balance a skilled athlete finds between mental focus, overall calm, and the energy needed to perform. In fact, performing vocally is an athletic endeavor.

Even when the vocalist is well-practiced and talented, the desired result for the song might come from a subtle shift of strategies involving the technologies for recording or processing the vocal, revealing even more magic in a performance. A skilled vocal producer listens for the "human connection" in the vocal performance. That could be passion, disdain, love, lust, being calm, being wild, whispering, screaming, and a plethora of other tricks and techniques that make a song sound oh-so-interesting to listen to, and that captures the listener.

Requests for breathy, chest voice, or nasal (twang) vocal qualities, for example, can make a song come alive in ways that the vocalist may not have realized. As an analogy, think of a professional sports coach who is active on the sidelines, drawing up plays as the game unfolds. While the team is well-practiced and talented, in the heat of the game, the coach views the performance through a more global lens with a specific outcome in mind.

This is why trusting the vocalist's process is so important. A great vocal producer nurtures and nudges these colors in a way that also supports the vocalist's technique and tolerances.

KNOWING AND UNDERSTANDING THE SONG

Many people write songs with guitar or piano, or in their DAW. The song has rhythm, melody, and harmony. The language of its lyrics has spoken punctuation and emotional expression, which lead to vocal and instrumental phrasing. Once the song is chosen for production, you would record the instrumentation and the scratch vocal (see chapter 7), and rerecord as needed until the song has become its best self. Early versions of the song can be an important part of what shapes the vocal performance—and ultimately, the production.

Members of the Magic Triangle can review the early recordings to offer their input as the song takes shape. When you know and understand what the song is about—every word, every breath—the performance is heightened. Everyone on the team should be on the same page with their knowledge of the lyrics, and their understanding of the song's *intention*. An analogy to this process is when an athlete and their coach review videos of their games and practices, to know their strengths and weaknesses, or when an actor studies their character's back story to understand what makes them tick.

Keep in mind that the stakeholders for the final production could be the self-producing artist, producer, vocal coach, recordist, mixing engineer, mastering engineer, publishing company, record company, angel investors, or distribution network—all of whom might wish to offer their suggestions. Any suggestions made during the production process can impact the recording. Caution: "too many cooks spoil the broth." A strong producer knows how to manage these varying opinions and interests and should have control over the project's direction, ideally in conjunction with the vocalist/artist.

CHAPTER 4

Shaping the Vocal Performance

This is the scenario. The vocalist stands at the mic, perhaps stretching their neck, back, and arms as they anticipate recording. Their heart may be racing, and they take another sip of water. They inhale deeply and slowly to steady their energy. They put on headphones and test their mic, and confirm that the balance of voice to tracks is good and that they can hear what they need in the mix. The track rolls, the song starts. They take in the song's tempo, rhythms, and key. They may move to the beat, while grounding their energy in legs and feet. They are passionate and ready to perform, visualizing the song and the reason they are standing there. Finally, they take in their first vocal breath, and begin the performance.

What has brought the vocalist to this moment? A great deal. Artistic development, ongoing work on their vocal instrument—possibly for many years, and likely sacrifices made by themselves and others have all contributed significantly to help them arrive here now.

If you are working on your own, you have spent time and money to get the best gear you can in order to create the best recording you can. You are focused and determined. Now, today, it's all about getting the very best vocal performance and recording quality that you can muster.

Your objective as producer or artist-producer is to reach your listener in a powerful and long-lasting way through the microphone in the medium of an indelible recording. You want the recorded vocal to be superbly expressive. When done well, the vocal will align with the song musically and lyrically to create a polished, finished piece of art. Let's begin with the story that will shape the vocal performance.

THE SONGS, STORYTELLING, AND INTENTION

When selecting the songs, think about what each song should convey emotionally. What is its message? What is your final objective for the recording, for the larger project? Who is your audience, your market? No matter what a song is about, one way or another, it's telling a story. Vocalists use words to shape the song's story, combining language, rhythm, melody, and nuance. Whether the song's melody is simple or complex, and whether the vocal is sung, spoken, or rap, the vocalist communicates feelings through the sound and quality of their voice. Their *intention* as they use their voice is what generates this feeling. Having intention means being clear about what they want to communicate, thinking and feeling those things, without ambiguity.

The role of the vocalist is to stay focused on the execution of the story, while the role of the vocal producer is to provide feedback on whether the delivery is hitting or missing the objective.

A recorded performance does not have to be a simple "live" capture. It is a document that cements a moment in time, using a process that, when done well, will be heard again and again.

A good story draws in the listener. For example, think about leaving someone a voice message. Did you nail it on the first try? Maybe not. "Oh, I can do better than that." What exactly do you want to say? So, you might try again so your attitude, message, and vibe come through. Each person leaving a voice message conveys something unique to them, and their intention is felt through their voice.

A vocalist being moved is what moves the audience.

UNDERSTANDING AND EXPRESSING THE LYRICS

A three-minute recording is an audio story. The audience wants to "see" the story in the song and the performance, and their senses are triggered by it. When the vocalist is clear about what they are feeling when performing the song or spoken work, they can embody it fully and express it naturally. The producer's job is to assess that communication. As you listen to them, can you imagine the touch, sights, sounds, or even the tastes and smells of the story? A well-produced story will give you an experience, especially when the vocalist is in touch with their intention for the song. The role of the vocal producer is to help them pull the listener into the experience.

Here are some questions to consider, and possible solutions:

- Does the vocalist have a clear understanding of and intention for the song, and are they connecting with it both thematically and emotionally? If not, it's helpful to spend time going through the words with them, one by one, to uncover the intention.
- Does each word have a *purpose* within the text? Suggest reading the lyrics first as if speaking to someone. What are they saying? If a word within a line doesn't add anything—such as connecting words like *and, if, so, but, the*—consider softening it, or even striking it, which can make a vocal more polished.
- Do the *breaths* make sense where they're taken? Do you say, "I like to eat piz-[breath]-za," with two breaths, or do you say, "I like to eat pizza" on one breath? Sometimes, vocalists take breaths within the text when they don't need them, either out of habit or by not focusing on the complete meaning of the phrase. Sometimes, too, the breath is intentionally part of the phrasing. Decide where the vocalist needs to breathe in order to complete a phrase, where breaths might be used stylistically, and if they should be audible.
- Will it add to a sung performance if the vocalist uses their speech pattern to perform the melody? Suggesting that the vocalist first speaks the words to the rhythm of the melody, and then sings them in that

speech-like way can introduce a more conversational, intimate moment into a song.

- Does the end of a phrase hold out on a pitch, and is it sung with a straight tone or with vibrato? Depending on the song, more interest can be added when there are various ends to phrases.
- Is the song memorized, known solidly backwards and forwards? This enables the vocalist to focus on the performance.
- Does the song need vocal ornamentations? Sometimes, melisma (carrying a sound across a few notes), bending down or up to a note, whoops, shouts, and little turns (mini trills) can add interest to a performance.
- Are the lyrics being pronounced well? Or are they hard to understand? Are they over-articulated or under-articulated?

Sometimes, lyrics don't make a lot of sense, or are repetitive. A strong performance comes from finding the gem within each line of text. Does the story have a plot? "She did this, he did that, they went here and said such-and-such." Or is it more of a free-flowing set of ideas or visualizations? "The sky is blue with billowing clouds, reflected in the ocean tide, as I lay here in the sand." The following questions are tools you and the vocalist can use as a starting point to uncover meaning in the song.

- Who are the characters in the song? Is the story a familiar one for the vocalist, or is the song about someone else's experience?
- What is the setting for the song: Indoors or outside? On a plane or in bed? Is it nighttime or day? Is it raining or sunny? Is the narrator in the tropics or in the snow? In a parking lot or at a dinner table? If there is no time or place in the lyrics, can the vocalist envision their own location as they perform?
- What is the story's central emotion? Is it joy or anger? Delight or jealousy? Passion or fear? Hurt or excitement? Boredom or love? Frustration or bliss? Excitement or boredom? Or does the song have more than one main emotion, mixing several feelings?
- Are the lyrics descriptive and poetic or obtuse and prosaic?
- Are the lyrics simple and repetitive? Or are they complex lyrics with infrequent repetition?
- Is there any hidden meaning in the lyrics or more than one way to interpret their meaning?

The vocalist is a kind of actor: their job is to highlight human experience through the sounds and cadence of their voice. By speaking the lyrics to practice their cadence, or speaking them along with the melody, personal expression can become more dramatic—even more so than how one would say these words in a conversation. The objective lies somewhere in between speaking and singing. The producer can enhance this expression by suggesting different vocal tones, such as breathy or clear, loud or soft, legato or staccato, and with or without vibrato.

Emotions are universal—we all know fear, love, hate, anger, elation, hope, despair, anticipation, and so on. When the expressed feelings are honest, and not held back—genuine emotion comes through. When it's a love song, for example, if the vocalist doesn't relate personally to the lyric, it doesn't matter whom the vocalist is thinking about—even their dog, or their younger sibling—because love is love, and that emotion will come through when it's sincere. Then, it's up to the listener to receive it. Once the expression is out there, the audience can take in the experience of the song and personalize it for themselves.

DESIGNING THE SONG

The job of the producer is to help the vocalist uncover their performance. Guiding the vocalist is comparable to a conductor asking the first violins in an orchestra to play ***ff*** (very loud) or ***pp*** (very soft) at specific sections of a composition. The conductor is the designer, the violinists are the experts in execution, and what the listener experiences is a teamwork of design and execution.

As we've said, working on songs in advance thoroughly will translate into the best results. A recorded vocal performance can have an intention and sound that might not have been evident to the vocal coach during preparation for the recording, nor evident to the A&R person or the producer of the record. However, a *vocal* producer—someone who knows the song and also knows how to work with and listen to the artist—can push and pull magic from a vocalist. What can the vocal producer do or say to achieve that magic? First, they need a working knowledge of the many different tones and sounds that a singer can produce to achieve storytelling and a desired intention.

Don't be afraid to experiment, and—depending upon the song's style—step away from established rules about what "sounds good." Create. Invent. And, to get this level of magic, treat the artist with respect and patience. It should always be "us against the world" in order for that conductor/first violins scenario to work well for the artist and vocal producer.

Also keep in mind that if after several unsuccessful takes the performance just isn't there yet, it's time to take a break. Give the vocalist and yourself a physical—and mental—break. What if the problem is the design? Perhaps the breaths are being taken after words four and six, but should really be taken after words five and eight, for example. Or, the agreed upon dynamics are taxing the vocalist, causing them to tire too easily. Don't be afraid to continue experimenting until you land upon a design that really helps the song come to life.

USING TIMBRE AND EXPRESSIVE VARIETY FOR STYLES

A vocalist stylizes a song by how they use their voice, breath, diction, tone, and vibrato. For some genres of music, a vocal that does not change timbre significantly from pitch to pitch is the hallmark of great vocal performance, such as traditional Western classical singing. In other styles, especially contemporary popular/commercial songs, varying timbre and vocal qualities is part of a nuanced performance. This is because many contemporary styles are intended to be as expressive as dramatic speech, rather than producing consistent, beautiful lines as in other genres. For example, the first verse might be sung with a breathy tone, the second verse with a medium clear tone, and the chorus with a strong belt. Using a range of tonal colors can help the song grow from quiet, to more intense, to loud and passionate. One example of this is Céline Dion's performance of "My Heart Will Go On" (theme song from *Titanic*, 1997). A nasal tone is also commonly heard in many styles such as pop, country, and R&B/hip-hop. Two great examples of a nasal tone are "How to Love" by Lil Wayne (2011) and "Wrecking Ball" by Miley Cyrus (2013).

The same song can be designed for a recording in radically different ways. Let's compare three versions of the song "Tutti Frutti," first recorded by Little Richard (1955, co-written with Dorothy LaBostrie), another recorded by Pat Boone, and a third by Elvis Presley—all within a few months of each other in 1955 and 1956. Both Little Richard and Elvis use a glottal, growl-like sound when they enter the song with "whop bop b-luma b-lomp bom bom." Pat Boone does not attempt this growl, in part perhaps to adjust the song for his audience, but also because that was not a normal or comfortable way for him to sing. Little Richard goes on to perform the word "Rudy" with a softer timbre than the preceding "tutti frutti" phrase. Pat Boone uses the exact same timbre for both phrases. Elvis, on the other hand, has a slightly exasperated-sounding downward scoop on the second syllable of "Rudy," with an obvious yodel-like upward scoop when he says "frutti," which is different from both Little Richard and Pat Boone. Listen to the three recorded versions of these performances side-by-side, and make note of the timbral variations explored by Little Richard and Elvis Presley, compared with the more consistent timbral delivery by Pat Boone. Were Little Richard, Elvis, and Pat Boone "just being themselves" when recorded? Or, perhaps their performances were produced in order to augment the recordings with articulated rhyming phrases, tempos, and timbres, going beyond how they sang the song live.

Another example is the Chainsmokers' song "Closer" (2016), featuring Andrew Taggart singing the male lead vocal and Halsey singing the female lead vocal. Andrew's phrasing sounds unexpressive, and many words have a slight edge as he slips easily into fry voice. (See chapter 3 for more information about vocal sounds and techniques.) Halsey enters her verse with a breathy tone that is also EQ'ed to match the timbre of Andrew's voice. (See chapter 6 for more on EQ.) Though she sings an octave higher than Andrew, she is in a lower part of her range, scooping into a higher register as she tightens and releases her voice on the words "moved" and "now," which provides a "glottal pop" effect.

Fast-forward to 2018, and Halsey's airy tone remains intact on "Without Me." In the chorus, Halsey sings, "Tell me how it feels sittin' up there" in a mix voice tone, which is bright and placed forward in the mouth. Singing the next words, "feeling so high but too far away to hold me," she flips out of her mix placement into head voice on the word "so" and then back into mix placement. While this is a common occurrence when a vocalist feels they're at the top part of their range and need to lighten their tone to sing a higher note, in this case, the lightening adds an interesting quality to the line. This mid-phrase register shift can be tricky to execute, and needs to be practiced. She sings with several textures throughout the song, including a fry-crunch sound when she sings the f-word in the prechorus.

Of the thousands of vocalists who deliver emotive and dynamic performances, Gladys Knight, Al Green, and Laura Nyro are worth their weight in gold as reference points that all vocalists and vocal producers can learn from. They create connections with their songs and their audiences not just because they have great voices, but also because of the vocal timbral arrangements they use. They swell up on a line, then swell down. They open up their projection (louder volume) and then pull it back. They articulate a word clearly and succinctly, then slur or mumble the next one. This timbral arrangement may happen even within a single phrase on one breath, offering significant dynamism, similar to a great actor reciting a soliloquy.

In "I'm Still in Love with You" by Al Green (1972), listen to the performance of "let you know-oo-ho," and "I look in your eye-i-i" in the middle of verse 1, where he flips between his expressive falsetto and lower voice; it is a clinic on timbre and a dynamic use of Modes 1 and 2. Next, listen to the low-volume delivery on the word "know" during the phrase "he's come to know" in "Midnight Train to Georgia" by Gladys Knight and the Pips (1973). Then listen to how Laura Nyro switches dramatically from a soft, gentle opening, quickly swooping upwards into a high mix on "whoa, you better hide your heart," then right away shifting to a strong middle range mix in the chorus of her classic opus "Eli's Coming" (1968). In track 33, a vocalist demonstrates a phrase using varying registers, dynamics, and tones for emotional expression.

33

Just as a saxophone player can study the phrasing nuances of Charlie Parker or John Coltrane and come up with their own playing style, vocalists and producers can mine great vocal performances for gems. While it's true that all voices are unique, and it can be hard to imagine emulating some well-received artists, using them as reference points is still very valuable for objectively studying their timbral arrangements.

USING TECHNIQUES SUCH AS VIBRATO, ENUNCIATION, AND SHORT/LONG NOTES

Vibrato is an oscillation of the vocal folds while holding a note, usually naturally occurring. Some people's vibrato is fast, for some it's slow, and others have barely any vibrato at all. An even and steady vibrato is an important aesthetic element in Western classical music as well as in popular musical theater styles, but not necessarily standard for popular contemporary styles. As you listen closely to popular songs, you can observe wide variations in how vocalists use vibrato. In classic jazz singing, a held note often starts out with straight tone, then releases into a somewhat wide and slow vibrato. In contemporary R&B singing, often the vibrato is "reversed," meaning pulled back into the throat and quickening, whereas classic R&B artists tend to release their natural vibrato while holding a note. Many pop and folk singers use no vibrato at all, or very little. And releasing vibrato while belting a high note in chest voice takes a great deal of skill. Understanding and using vibrato, even with varying speeds, is a technique that can be learned with a skilled instructor. Listen to track 34 to hear examples of straight tone and vibrato.

34

Enunciation refers to how words are pronounced; diction refers to the overall clarity of speech. How we enunciate vowels determines the timbre of the voice, while consonants provide articulation. You may see a video performance where the vocalist is barely opening their mouth, but if they perform that way in the studio, their diction, enunciation, articulation—and healthy vocal production—would likely be less effective. Good vocal production focuses on the voice performance, while good video production focuses on the visual performance, and they may not correlate.

Vowels are pitched tones that determine vocal timbre, intonation, and style. They may be adjusted for a regional accent or musical genre. For healthy vocal production, vowels are opened on higher pitches to reduce straining. Track 35 has some brief examples of how pronunciation can be modified and also shape vocal timbre.

35

Flat vowels like "ah" and "awe" tend to lower intonation. Peaking vowels like "ee" and "I" tend to raise intonation.

Vowels may be modified such as saying "fly" like "flah" instead of "fly-ee," or saying "night" like "naht" instead of "ni-eet."

When singing "mine," the long "i" sound might be changed to the short "a" sound as in "back," sounding more like "mahn."

To soften the long ee at the end of word "baby," it can be pronounced in several ways, such as "bay-beh," "bay-b ....ee," "bay-bay," or "bay-buh."

When belting a high note that ends in an "e" sound such as the word "me," the vowel "e" needs to be open to more of an "eh" sound, which also eliminates a constricted and strained production.

Consonant Key

CONSONANT	AS IN THE WORDS	QUALITY
B*	boy, baby, bat, scab	Lips seal then burst open with air
Ch	chair, charge, cherry, such	Similar to "Sh" but with a harder onset
D	dad, deal, seed	Tongue presses against front teeth with a burst of air
F	flower, fine, scarf	Air blows quickly against bottom lip and top teeth
G or J (soft)	jewel, gem, giant, hedge	Tongue and teeth seal then open quickly with a burst of air
G (hard)	good, great, lug	Back of the tongue comes up to close the pharynx then releases with a burst of air
H	hair, howl, hide	The only open consonant, air is pushed through an open vocal fold (abducted)
K	thick, shack, like, kite	Produced in the back of the throat, tongue presses up against the soft palate with a soft burst of air
L	love, lie, real, royal	Tongue presses up against front of hard palate in phonation
M	mom, may, mighty, same, time	Lips close, sound vibrates in the open space of the pharynx
N	nice, nasty, mine, run	Similar to "M" but the closure is from the tongue against the hard palate and lips don't close
P*	paper, pool, soup, lip	Lips press together and release with a burst of air
R	ready, run, car, star	Tongue is held in contraction in the middle of the mouth, while frequencies ring upwards through the hard palate
S	sexy, see, eyes, saves	Tongue creates a valve near the front teeth as air is pressed through the constricted opening
Sh	shut, shout, push, fish	Front of mouth is partially closed as air is pressed forward
T*	time, tell, pout, about	Tongue presses against the front teeth explosively with a burst of air
V	vain, vogue, rave, love	Top teeth buzz lightly against bottom lip
W	why, went, few, how	Lips pucker and release during phonation, sometimes with a small burst of air ("wh")
X	x-ray, extra, flex, exactly	Produced from the back of the throat, this is actually three sounds blended quickly, "eh" + "K" + "S"
Y	baby, why, sky, may	Sounds as "ee" at ends of words; or, the letter sound, as in "why," is a diphthong: "wah-ee"
Z	zebra, razzle-dazzle	Tongue is pressed against hard palate behind teeth during strong phonation

*Common plosives

Consonants are non-pitched sounds that enable us to articulate language. In many contemporary styles, over-articulating can sound too formal. Formally trained vocalists may need to soften their diction, including how they pronounce consonants at the *ends* of words. Consonants are also used for accents and syncopation. Track 36 demonstrates some examples.

36

Say the word "that" with a faint "T" at the end, rather than a crisp one. Then say the word "pretty" with a soft "P" at the start of the word, sounding more like "britty." Practice saying "beautiful" with a softer "B."

Try reciting the line "yeah reck-a-less behavior" from the chorus of "Pillowtalk" by Zane (2016), where "reckless" is sung with three syllables rather than two, enabled by the three consonants "R," "Ck," and "L."

For a deeper look at consonants and vowels, refer to *Your Singing Voice: Contemporary Techniques, Expression and Spirit* (Gagné, Berklee Press).

Short and Long Notes. Singers often love to hold out notes (legato). But many styles need rhythmic singing with short, staccato articulation. Some words simply need to end quickly, more like one would speak them. Blending long notes with short ones can be an effective way to bring contrast into a performance. "Every Summertime" by NIKI (2022) is a useful example of using mainly staccato singing in the verses, and legato lines in the prechoruses and choruses. An example of using very long notes at the end of each phrase, without vibrato, is "The Reason" by Hoobastank (2003). An example of verses sung very short then long by two artists in a duet is "Never Felt So Alone" by Labrinth with Billie Eilish (2023). Listen to track 37 to hear a phrases sung both legato and staccato.

37

DYNAMICS

The term *dynamics* refers to volume. Including dynamic variations throughout a song is hugely important for effective expression. When we speak, we have a range of dynamic highs and lows, even within one phrase. How you stress a word can change its meaning and emotional context.

Coach the vocalist to bring dynamic variations to their performance, using nuances to draw out even more emotional expression than is typical for speaking. This brings in and touches the listener. What is the context? For example, they could use an *intimate voice* in one section, followed by a *projected voice* in another. In this way, the song begins softly, as if they're speaking right next to someone's ear, then gets loud, as if trying to be heard across a crowded room. Even within one melodic passage or line, a big change in dynamics can add a great deal of character and nuance, such as a phrase that begins with a bright loud riff, then lands low in the range on a soft note—all on one breath.

The artist examples of timbre mentioned earlier in this chapter also demonstrate dynamic interpretation. In track 38, you can hear a phrase sung:

38

1. soft and clear
2. louder and clear
3. projected and belted

STYLISTIC HABITS

It's important for the vocalist to be aware of their stylistic habits. When someone who is trained in musical theater sings a pop song without adjusting stylistically, for example, the outcome may not work for the song. The same issue can apply if a country singer tries to sing jazz, or if a gospel singer takes on EDM, or if a folk singer tries to rap. Some well-known artists have stepped out of their familiar genre to sing what was happening musically at the time, and that doesn't always work out well. One example is when disco was king, many major artists at the time came out with a disco record—and they fell flat. It's difficult to change singing styles and habits, and a vocalist who can sing authentically in many different genres is rare indeed. Linda Ronstadt stands out as one artist who pulled this off. After forging a career as a major rock star, she shifted successfully to other genres (against the strong advice of her management) by singing Gilbert and Sullivan on Broadway, releasing the classic American Songbook album *What's New* (1983) that reached #2 on the jazz charts, and honoring her Mexican roots with the album *Canciones de Mi Padre* (1987).

As a producer, maintaining an objective ear with the vocalist can help them to observe when they are falling back into stylistic habits. For some vocalists, depending on their training and experience, it may be hard to recognize what those habits are. The producer can point out conscious choices to help find stylistic shifts such as vibrato, enunciation, and the length of held notes. A self-producing vocalist may struggle with this more than with a collaborative Magic Triangle team. If so, be mindful to use self-objectivity as a consistent part of your toolkit.

MOVEMENT WHILE RECORDING

Movement helps expression, because music *is* movement. Singing, especially, is movement because the vocalist's whole body is part of their instrument. So, if their body is stiff, their singing will be stiff, too. Encourage them to move some at the mic, for knees to bend and their face to express, so they aren't limiting their performance by holding perfectly still. Holding still usually tells the unconscious body that it's not safe, which in turn makes singing less free, more anxious, and more difficult. Although the vocalist still needs to pay attention to mic technique, including distance from the mic and not making sounds with their feet, that doesn't mean they have to be rigid. Suggest opening arms wide to the side, as if greeting a close friend. Pause the recording throughout the session for stretching stiff muscles. Suggest that they move to the groove at the mic, letting the rhythms guide the body from head to toe. Remind the vocalist to feel their legs and feet and be aware of how they're standing, feeling grounded. This whole-body awareness and freedom will make a noticeable difference in their phrasing, vocal health, and overall performance.

What should the vocalist move to? Most commonly, they should listen to the bottom end of the instrumentation to hear the groove: the kick (bass) drum and the bass guitar (or double bass). Grooves have subdivisions they can move to and lock into vocally, such as the common straight-eighths subdivision for 4/4 pop-rock grooves, a swinging eighths subdivision for jazz, or a busier groove with straight sixteenths such as hip-hop or funk. They can step to the downbeats while tracking the backbeats with a quiet tap of their hand.

Practical Session Notes for Producer and Vocalist

1. Come to the recording space already well warmed up, but don't over-practice beforehand. Save that big moment for the mic.
2. Sing the song in an easier manner, with less volume and intensity, while the team sets up the session, or during band rehearsal. This is called "marking," and will save your voice for the recording. Don't whisper though, as this is bad for your voice.
3. Keep some healthy snacks around.
4. It's natural to feel nervous and excited. Channeling this excitement away from nerves and negative thinking will give the vocal a zap of wonderful energy and enhance the performance.
5. Keep in mind that because the body changes somewhat day to day, so will the voice. It's normal for the vocalist to be a little inconsistent from one session to another.
6. Posture matters, and slouching or rolling shoulders forward inhibits breathing. If the vocalist leans on one leg and their hip leans outward, they'll be off balance, and this will affect their singing. They should make ample room for their ribs and midsection to expand upon inhalation, while keeping air in the body longer for support.
7. Scrunching up the face or furrowing the eyebrows indicates facial tension. Facial muscles have a direct impact on how the voice works, and a tense face makes singing harder. This might happen when going for a high note, a raw emotional sound, or a phrase that passes through a register shift. Tension in the face can also occur when feeling concerned about singing properly or effectively. Try tapping the center of the forehead gently while singing to release tension there. It works!
8. Bend the knees at the moment when singing a "high" note. The body goes down as the note goes up. It works!

CHAPTER 5

Creating Vocals Within the Stereo Field

Recording is like painting a picture. You record into an artificial medium that captures the natural world and modifies it for future playback. Before you set up your microphone, and before you record—understanding how to create a sonic tapestry by the use and placement of multiple vocals will enhance your vocal production significantly. Note that as you read this chapter, the various vocal positions described within the stereo field (localization) can best be heard without any added effects (such as reverb or delay), until your listening becomes a bit more advanced.

YOUR BRAIN INTERPRETS SOUND

Your brain is the primary organ used to translate the pressure variations of sound (vibrations) that your ears receive. In the natural world, you can perceive sound in all directions: front, back, left, right, up, and down. With recorded music, you hear audio as a flat representation of front, back, left, right, up, and down. This is called the *stereo field,* which is perceived while listening to two audio monitors (speakers) or headphones. You are hearing an artificial impression of the natural world. The DAW you record into distributes audio through its left and right outputs as a representation of the stereo field.

First, let's assume that you are always listening with two ears. So, you will eliminate scenarios where only one earphone is sending music to one ear for this discussion. When you listen to one speaker playing music centered directly in front of you, you are hearing a *monaural* (mono) audio signal. You can hear the frequency response (differing pitches) and the amplitude variations (differing levels) of the audio signals (e.g., vocal performances) passing through that one speaker. This was the common method of listening to recorded music from the 1920s to the late 1950s.

THE THREE DIMENSIONS OF THE STEREO FIELD

In 1957, after decades of experimentation dating back to the 1930s, *stereophonic (stereo)* sound debuted. Using two speakers positioned equidistantly to the left and to the right, stereo sound offered frequency response, amplitude variation, and a new perspective—panoramic locations. This is where the term "panning" comes from.

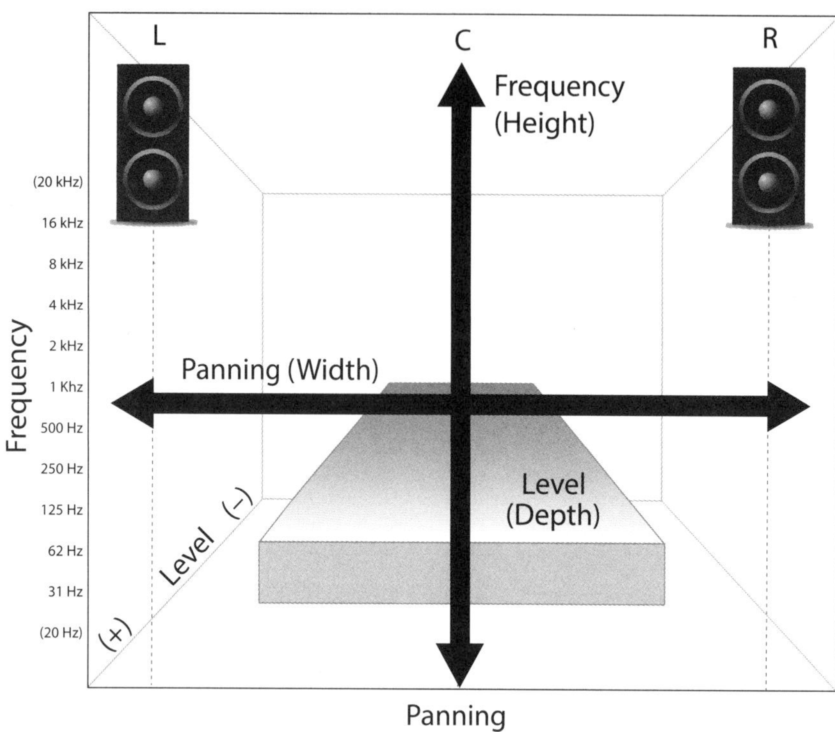

FIG. 5.1. Stereo Field Visual Representation

The pan pots (potentiometers) you use within the stereo field can be represented as a clock face, with 8 o'clock representing extreme left, 12 o'clock representing center, and 4 o'clock representing extreme right.

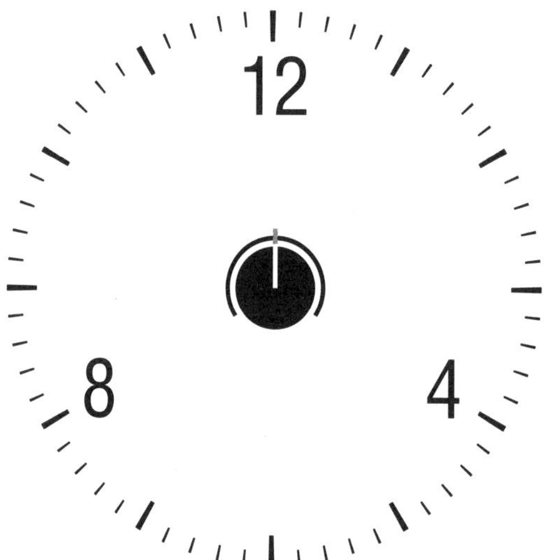

FIG. 5.2. Clock Face Representing a Pan Pot

Your brain is totally responsible for your perception of the 12 o'clock center signal because, of course, there is no center speaker—just left and right, unlike in the natural world, where we hear sound omnidirectionally. The center signal is actually a phantom center that doesn't really exist. It is a psycho-acoustic phenomenon created by your brain when the same sound arrives at both ears at the same time.

Mix Placement

After years of '60s and '70s producers experimenting with the lead vocal on the left, on the right, or in the center of the stereo field (attempts that were trying to mimic classical music hall sound locations), it became common practice in modern recordings to place lead vocals in the phantom center (12 o'clock). The vast majority of contemporary recordings place the lead vocal in this phantom center location.

Pan Law

When you pan your vocal left or right, you are invoking a mixing principle called the *pan law* (or pan rule). *Decibels* (dB) are an objective measurement of voltage, and manipulating decibel levels changes the perceived amplitude, or volume, for what you hear coming from the outputs of your DAW. Each increase of 6 dB doubles the voltage, sounding louder. Each decrease of 6 dB halves the voltage, sounding softer. Because there is no center signal, the center position is actually a sum of the left and right signals. It will be -3 dB lower than when panned extreme left or right. When you pan the vocal to the extreme left or right, it boosts the vocal by 3 dB to the side you have moved it. This *attenuation* (lowering of amplitude or sound) in the center creates the illusion of *equal power* panning when you sweep from left to center to right.

Equal power is a good thing. It helps your audio to sound even when you pan from left to right. Without the pan law, your performance in the phantom center would sound much louder, and your left and right signals would sound much lower. There are other level variations for the pan law, but -3 dB (equal power) is the most common settings preference in DAWs.

The importance of mix placement and the pan law are useful when mixing or playing back a single vocal, but they are even more helpful for creative record making when there are multiple vocal performances in your song.

USING MULTIPLE VOCALS CREATIVELY

Before you being recording, let's look at some ideas that can help to make a lead vocal have more presence in the recording. Adding vocals in support of the lead vocal contributes pitch, level, timing, and chorusing (modulation) variations. Keep in mind that whether you add a simple unison double of the lead, or lush background vocals filling up the stereo field, all vocals need to be panned and balanced intentionally.

Let's explore some techniques for arranging multiple vocal tracks in your recording.

Unison Doubling

Unison doubling is an interesting effect that "fattens" the lead vocal. It takes advantage of slight natural variations in pitch and time between a first and second performance that are both singing the same part simultaneously, in the same octave. The second performance is usually recorded to match an existing word, phrase, or full performance of the lead vocal. This is called a *natural* double. The slight differences between the two performances creates a chorusing effect that many producers use for words, phrases, or a full vocal performance. You can hear an example of this effect in the first prechorus (:50) of "Déjà Vu" by Olivia Rodrigo (2021).

Natural unison doubling is not an identical copy of a vocal performance. If the second vocal were identical, it would merely raise the level of the original performance by 6.02 dB (a doubling of voltage). The whole point of unison doubling is to create a chorusing effect, not just a volume boost. How does this work? By way of example, imagine playing an A440 sine tone and sing an A441 against it, you will hear one pulse of modulation. A442 would result in two pulses, and so on. If you sing A439 against A440, you will also get one pulse of variation. A438 would result in two pulses and so on. The pulsing between the notes is the natural modulation between the difference of the pitches. This is the chorusing effect.

39

In track 39, you can hear:

1. a sine tone at 440 Hz
2. two sine tones at 440 Hz (which raises the volume by 6 dB)
3. a sine tone at 440 Hz and a sine tone at 441 Hz (modulating one cycle/second sharp)
4. a sine tone at 440 Hz and a sine tone at 439 Hz (modulating one cycle/second flat)

Notice that examples (3) and (4) of track 39 sound very similar.

40

In track 40, you can hear:

1. a sine tone at 440 Hz
2. a sine tone at 440 Hz and a sine tone at 450 Hz (sharp)
3. a sine tone at 440 Hz a sine tone at 430 Hz (flat)

41

In track 41, you can hear:

1. a solo vocal phrase
2. the phrase and one identical copy (sounds louder)
3. a natural double recording of the phrase (sounds slightly different)

A second, *artificial* way to create a vocal double, rather than rerecording the performance a second time, is to shift the timing of an identical copy of the lead vocal. This can be done by copying the audio to another track and shifting the copy by 30 to 60 ms (milliseconds), or by sending the original performance, via a Bus Send, to an Aux (auxiliary) track containing a mono delay. Set the delay to 100 percent wet, and the delay time to 30 to 60 ms. Now, raise the Bus Send until what you hear matches the level of the lead vocal. The result will sound like a double, though less realistic than a natural double.

42

In track 42, you can hear:

1. a solo vocal phrase
2. an artificial double of the phrase (the original phrase was copied/pasted and then delayed by 30 ms using a digital delay)

Even though artificial doubles are an option, natural doubles are the preferred method for fattening vocals. They are usually done by the same vocalist that performed the lead vocal, though there are times when duos double each other, as in "I Love It" by Icona Pop (2016). Even though doubling is an interesting effect, be careful that you don't overuse it, because it tends to (1) minimize the intimacy of a vocal performance, and (2) skew the articulation of the vocal performance.

When should you use a unison double? That depends on your creative ideas and what you want to hear in the recording. Try it for different phrases in your song to see what you like; once you can recognize the sound, listen to where contemporary producers use the concept in their work.

Unison Triples

Another popular multiple vocal technique for lead vocals is unison triples. Natural unison triples are three matching performances of a word, phrase, or full performance, where one is panned left, one is panned right, and the dominant performance is panned in the center. The stereo field localization of these three positions is what makes it interesting, unique, and totally different from unison doubling. While there is only modulation occurring in a unison double, *localization* (for which the listener can hear a distinct voice in each of the three locations) is the distinguishing feature of a unison triple. Unison triples work well when panned all the way to 8 o'clock, 12 o'clock, and 4 o'clock, because these positions leave the center available for the dominant lead vocal to stand out. Bringing the left and right vocals closer to the center narrows the stereo field, and is a bit less intriguing, but there are no handcuffs to your personal creativity.

You can hear this effect in the choruses of "Wrecking Ball" by Miley Cyrus (2013), or the prechoruses and choruses of "Levitating" by Dua Lipa (2020). In the song "Little Freak" by Harry Styles (2022), the double and triple vocals are panned far left and far right, with a softer lead vocal placed center.

Although the result in "Little Freak" may sound a lot like a split-double (one vocal planned left, one panned right, and no vocal in the center), it is actually a unison triple. A true split-double loses the vocal focus in the center of the recording, it is used less frequently in multi-vocal production concepts.

43

In track 43, you can hear:

1. a solo vocal phrase panned center
2. a sung double of the phrase panned left and right (a split-double)
3. a sung triple of the phrase panned left, center, and right
4. the same sung triple with the centered pan volume lowered

Centered Harmonies

Anything that can be done with a lead vocal can be done with a harmony relative to the lead vocal performance. Anywhere from one, two, three—or more—harmony parts can be placed in the center of the mix alongside the lead vocal. This can work when they are leveled so they don't clobber the lead. On "Rocket" by Beyoncé (2013), you can hear the lead vocal in the center, and a three-part harmony that joins it with all of its notes also panned to the center on the line, "don't take your eyes off it" (0:23). Because in this example the harmonies are lower in the mix than Beyoncé's lead vocal, and are performed differently, Beyoncé's lead remains the focal point of the song.

In the case where there is only one voice on a harmony part, placing in the center supports the lead vocal without feeling out of balance. Listen to an example of this in the chorus of "Forever After All" by Luke Combs (2021). Or, if you only have single voices performing harmony parts—no matter how many harmonies there are—when you place them in the center as well, it will help your record to sound harmonically balanced in the center.

44

In track 44, you can hear a solo vocalist perform:

1. a sung tonic (root) note
2. a note sung a major third above (the third)
3. a note sung a minor third above that (the fifth)
4. a centered triad with all three notes sounding together as a chord

45

In track 45, you can hear a trio performing:

1. a tenor singing a phrase panned center
2. an alto singing the phrase one third above panned center
3. a soprano singing the minor third above that (the fifth) panned center
4. a triad panned center with all three notes sounding together as a chord

Left and Right Spread Harmonies

A common practice is to perform each harmony note twice, then pan them evenly left and right. This allows the focus to remain on the lead vocal performance in the center. You can hear Finneas using this effect in "I love You" by Billie Eilish (2019), when he sings her melody an octave lower, doubles it, and then pans one left and one right. In the chorus of "Say So" by Doja Cat (2019), this effect is used in parallel fourths against her melody, also panned left and right. Jazmine Sullivan's "Pick Up Your Feelings" (2021) uses this effect as three-part harmony, on the word "feelings" in the chorus (0:54).

Stacking Background Harmonies

As outlined, you can place harmonies to a lead vocal in the center, or spread left and right. In these configurations, you can also double the harmonies to make the background vocals sound even richer. Consider the following popular choices.

If the root, third, and fifth of the vocal harmony are panned to the center, and perform the same line as the lead vocal, harmonic color is added but without the interest created by stereo imaging. This placement also forces the lead vocal to fight the backgrounds for focus from the listener. Again, Beyoncé's "Rocket" is an example of this being done successfully because of careful level adjustments that allow the lead vocal to shine.

If the root, third, and fifth of the vocal harmony are *cascaded*—where one is on the left, one is on the right, and one is in the center—this creates an unbalanced listening experience because different harmonies hit each ear. You also have to decide which note will fight for the center image along with the lead vocal. You can hear this effect on many older recordings, like the chorus in "Jamming" by Bob Marley (1977).

46

In track 46, you can hear:

1. a sung phrase panned center
2. the same phrase sung a third above panned left
3. the same phrase sung a fifth above panned right
4. a cascaded triad with all three panned harmony notes sounding together as a chord

If the root, third, and fifth of the harmony are each doubled, you can pan each note left and right. The result will be a complete 1, 3, 5 harmony on both sides of the stereo field, leaving the phantom center for the lead vocal. This is a great use of background vocals that you hear on many contemporary songs, such as in the chorus of "Positions" by Ariana Grande (2020).

47

In track 47, you can hear:

1. a tonic note panned left
2. a third panned left
3. a fifth panned left
4. the triad with all three notes panned left, sounding together as a chord
5. a tonic panned right
6. a third panned right
7. a fifth panned right
8. the triad with all three notes panned right, sounding together as a chord
9. both left and right stacks sounding together as a left and right spread harmony stack

48

If the root, third, and fifth of the vocal harmony are each tripled, you can also pan each harmony left, center, and right, as demonstrated in track 48. The result is a complete harmony on the left, center, and right of the stereo field. This can be a viable use of background vocals, but it does obscure the center imaging focus that the lead vocal needs. This technique is often used when the backgrounds are more dominant than the lead vocal. It can be done for a momentary phrase or for an entire section. The chorus of "No Plans for Love" by D Nice with Ne-Yo and Kent Jones (2021) is a good example.

If the root, third, and fifth of the vocal harmony are each quadrupled, you can create a rich chorusing effect for each note on the left and right of the stereo field. This is a popular multiple-background vocal technique, that most contemporary vocal producers have in their arsenals, for fattening choruses within the stereo field. You can also hear it during several other song sections in "Wonder" by Shawn Mendes (2020), "Damage" by H.E.R. (2021), "Leave the Door Open" by Bruno Mars, Anderson Paak, and Silk Sonic (2021); the end chorus of "drivers' license" by Olivia Rodrigo (2021); and on hundreds of contemporary hit songs.

49

In track 49, you can hear a quadruple built with four independently sung triads:

1. a triad panned left
2. a triad doubled with both panned left
3. a third triad panned right
4. a third triad doubled with both panned right
5. all four triads sounding together

50

Many vocal producers record no more than two voices per note, per panning position within the stereo field (left, center, and right). This is because if you record more than two identical unison tracks and pan them to the same position, the sound becomes clustered and less clear. Track 50 contains one vocal phrase that was sung for a total of six times, all panned center, demonstrating natural clustering with less clarity. While this effect is subtle when isolated, it becomes apparent when other instruments are placed in the same plane of the stereo field with your unison stack.

When a vocal part is copied, pasted, and placed in the same panning position, with each copy shifted a small amount, not only is the sound clustered and less clear, comb filtering can result. Comb filtering is a drastic alteration of the vocal resonance, and can make the vocals sound metallic. So, when you want to add more than two voices and use the same panning position for the additional voices, it's helpful to change the timbre of those additional voices instead. For example, use a different vocal quality in unison on the same note. This will minimize the comb-filtering effect.

51

Track 51 contains one recorded phrase that has been copied, pasted, and shifted five times by 7 milliseconds (ms) each. From the original, the first copy is shifted by 7 ms, the second by 14 ms, the third by 21 ms, the fourth by 28 ms, and the fifth by 35 ms. All phrases are panned center, demonstrating the true comb-filtering effect. (You can really hear the metallic sound on the breathing in between notes.)

Ad Libs

Vocal *ad libs* (from *ad libitum*, "at one's pleasure"), which are intended to sound like they happened in the moment and "free," may in fact be prepared in advance. Skilled vocalists relish the opportunity to show their vocal skills using ad lib melodic interpretation.

There are three ways to imbed ad libs into your song:

- They can be part of the performance using *melodic interpretation* at will, such as in "When I Was Your Man" by Bruno Mars (2012) or "Someone You Loved" by Lewis Capaldi (2019). The ad libs are performed as variations to the stated melodies presented in previous sections of the song.
- They can be performed *in counterpoint* with the lead vocal performance in unison or in harmony with an existing lead vocal, such as "I'm Every Woman" by Chaka Khan (1978). Singing them in counterpoint reveals a timbre, timing, and pitch that do not have to be fully in sync with the lead vocal. You can hear this done well in the third chorus (2:14) of "We're Good" by Dua Lipa. There is also a harmony in the third verse on the line "like I knew you would" (2:01), which may have been performed on the ad lib track, but is actually a synchronized harmony to the lead vocal. It is similar to an ad lib but has no improvisational feel.
- *Call-and-response* is another ad lib approach that is very popular and easy to recognize. The recorded lead vocal performs its phrase as the "call," and the ad lib performs a "response" using a complementary phrase, or vice versa. Call-and-response can also be performed between lead vocals and background vocals and choirs. You can hear this effect at the beginning of "Peaches" by Justin Bieber (2021). The timbre of the response is slightly band-pass filtered (like a telephone sound) in order to maintain its unique character apart from the lead vocal.

Timing and Phrasing Alignment

When working with multiple-vocal techniques, it is important to lock the timing of consonants that begin and end phrases. If this is difficult, you can keep the consonant on the first vocal of the stack and soften the consonant for successive performances. You can also use your DAW to cut and move, or TCE the consonants (Time, Compression, and Expansion—see chapter 9), so that they are more aligned. Another technique is for the vocalist(s) to soften the ends of words, so only one or two recorded takes articulates the ending consonant of a word clearly.

52

Track 52 contains a tripled phrase that is:

1. performed with uneven timing of the *beginning* consonants, and
2. performed with even timing of the *beginning* consonants.

53

Track 53 contains a tripled phrase that is:

1. performed with uneven timing of the *ending* consonants, and
2. performed with even timing of the *ending* consonants.

Make sure also to monitor the articulation of the vocalist(s) vowels. A Boston-pronounced "pahk," and a New York-pronounced "pawrk" (both are saying "park") might sound strange together. Although regional variation is fine for the lead vocalist, background vocalists should pronounce words in the same way for consistency in their tones, often matching the lead vocalist when doubling their line.

Keep Breaths Coordinated

Breaths are an important part of a vocal performance, and managing breathing for singing is a fundamental part of vocal technique. Managing breathing for multiple vocals is especially important, because hearing breaths from several takes can add too much extra noise. Work with the vocalist(s) to map out coordinated breaths that work with the phrasing and lyrics. Considering whether you want to hear the breaths or edit them out, is personal preference and up to your creative interpretation.

The first vocal pass in a series of background vocals needs to be well-designed, which sets up the breathing patterns for all the vocals to follow. In this way, the breaths in multiple vocals will align.

Often, breaths occur at a place of punctuation such as a comma or period, so as not to break up a lyrical phrase. Audible breaths may also be used as a stylistic or rhythmic component. In Michael Jackson's "Beat It" (1982), the breaths are not audible in the background, only in his lead vocal. In Halsey's "Without Me" (2018), you can hear the background breaths periodically. An audible inhalation can also add intimacy, such as when multiple vocals sing softly and are close mic'ed. One example is "I Love You" by Billie Eilish (2019).

54

Track 54 contains a tripled phrase with uncoordinated followed by coordinated breaths:

1. with uneven timing of the inhaled breath sounds that don't match, and
2. with coordinated timing of the inhaled breath sounds that match.

The techniques provided in this chapter will help as you consider creative options for the performances within your song and the stereo field. Some songs and genres need only a lead vocal performance. Other songs and genres may use additional vocal performances as "ear candy" to augment timbre, timing, and pitch for broadening the listening experience. You are the one who chooses which technique(s) work best for your project.

Let's dig in and start recording!

CHAPTER 6

Preparing to Record

Since the invention of the phonograph by Thomas Edison in 1877, recording audio has been a mechanical representation of real life. By definition, recording captures what was real into an artificial medium. Recording is not real life: it is analogous, meaning similar, to real life. This is where the audio term "analog" came from. Analog recording matured over the decades through a series of mediums, until the mid-fifties rock and roll era, when magnetic tape and large-format consoles dominated professional recording. Digital technology first appeared in the 1970s, and evolved through the 1980s as music sequencers, drum machines, MIDI, and other digital devices became standardized for the record producer. Meanwhile, magnetic tape and the large-format consoles persisted.

Our modern digital recording technology is the descendant of Thomas Edison's analog recording technology. It was in the early 2000s that the DAW (digital audio workstation) ascended to dominance as the standard professional recording format, while maintaining terms and concepts borrowed from analog recording. Most of you reading this book will be using a DAW to record your projects. Your DAW contains more processing power than Edison could dream of harnessing, yet with a much smaller physical footprint.

THE VOCAL PRODUCTION PATH

Let's take a look at the recording and playback paths of your workflow.

Consider the recording path of vocal production in the digital realm:

- Sources: acoustic performance that you wish to record
- Recording spaces: rooms in which you are recording
- Transducers: microphones that convert the voice's acoustical energy into electrical energy (analog signal)
- A/D (analog to digital) conversion: audio interface that converts the electrical energy (recorded vocal performance) into a digital signal
- Modifiers: equalizers, compressors, and time-based effects that alter the incoming vocal signal

- Routers: cables, sends, busses, and auxiliary faders that move the vocal from one point to another
- Recording medium: hard drives with as fast a speed, and as large a capacity, as you can afford to store the recorded vocal performance

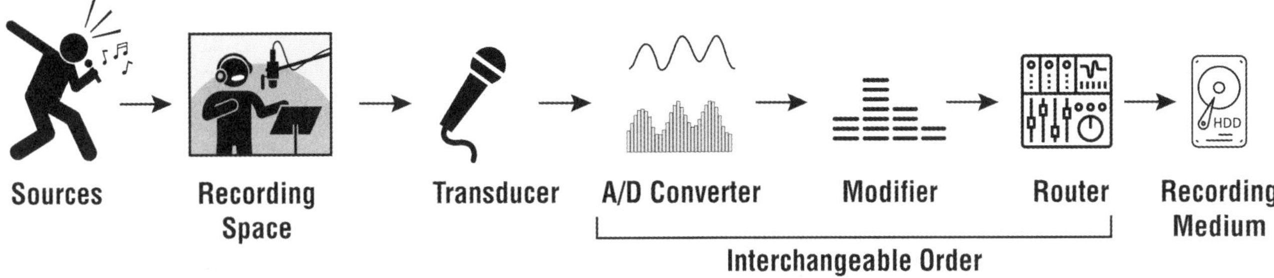

FIG. 6.1. Recording Path: Analog to Digital

Also consider the playback path:

- Playback medium: retrieving the stored vocal for playback
- Routers: moving the vocal to the desired output points in the playback system
- Modifiers: altering the outgoing vocal signal's level, equalization, and time-based effects
- D/A (digital to analog) conversion: audio interface converts the digital signal (recorded vocal performance) into electrical energy
- (Reverse) Transducers: loudspeakers (monitors) converting electrical energy into acoustical energy (we will talk about headphones and earbuds in chapter 7)
- Listening spaces: rooms where you critically listen to the playback of the voice
- Ears/brain: perceiving, critiquing, and enjoying the recorded performance

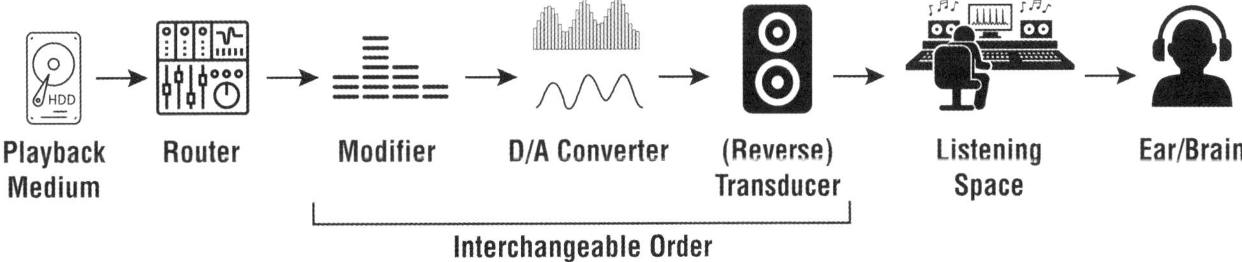

FIG. 6.2. Playback Path: Digital to Analog

The vocal producer needs to pay attention to each stage of the recording and playback paths. This creates a transparent process from one stage to the next, that doesn't interfere with your creativity. And, if something should go wrong, you want to be able to troubleshoot its location along the signal flow path.

RECORDING SPACES

Your recording space has an impact on the recorded performance. When recording with a live band, for example, the vocalist may be in the same room (and ideally isolated by gobos), which can create an immediate experience with the band, or the vocalist can be in a separate booth with its own door. If the tracks are prerecorded with MIDI, the vocalist could also be in a separate vocal booth, or in the control room with the producer/recordist. When the vocalist and producer are in separate spaces, remember to check in frequently over a talkback mic to keep the vocalist "in the loop" to prevent a drain of needed energy and focus. Depending on the comfort level of the vocalist, working in the same space can foster more intimate communication. For all scenarios, sound isolation will help you get a clean vocal track.

All recording spaces reflect sound off of walls, ceilings, and floors. Multiple reflections create reverberance, which we also know as *reverb*. When a space is overly reverberant, multiple reflections might be printed onto your vocal track, which cannot be removed in the mix. Think of how your voice sounds in a bathroom, which is a small space. Or, how your voice sounds in an empty warehouse, a large space. Both of these spaces, if not treated, would add the ambiance of these rooms to your recording.

FIG. 6.3. Well-Treated Home Recording Space (Provided by Whisperroom, Courtesy of Betheny Zolt)

For example, wood and concrete reflect more sound than carpeting. A treated room will have absorbing or diffusing (redirecting) materials to mitigate the reflective energy of the walls, ceiling, and floor. *Absorbers* can range from heavy rugs to specially designed acoustic material capable of actively or passively absorbing reflections. *Diffusers* can range from egg cartons to intricately designed acoustic paneling capable of redirecting reflections away from your recording source.

A quick rule of thumb is to think of absorbing low frequencies and diffusing high frequencies. If you're on a budget, a treated space might take some experimenting but is worth looking into. Simple room dividers—like folding screens or acoustically treated *gobos* (movable acoustic isolation panels)—will help you reconfigure an overly reverberant room.

If your space is larger than 400 square ft., such as a 20 ft. by 20 ft. square room (37 square meters), or one that has a ceiling in excess of 20 ft. (6 meters), it will definitely need to be treated.

A mic gobo will mitigate room reflections, and can be helpful for vocal performances that are performed close to the mic.

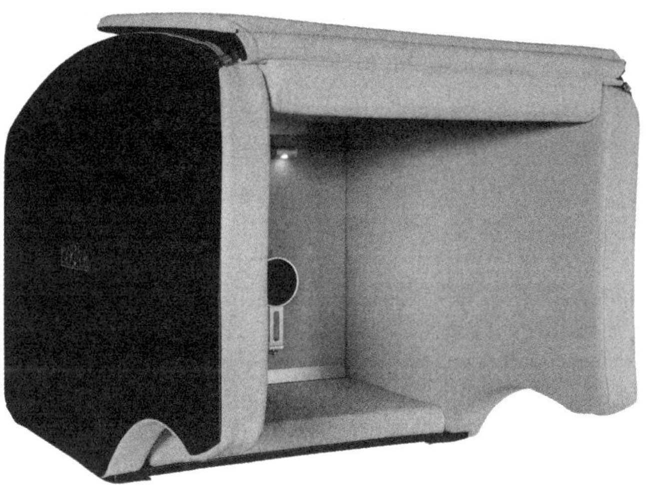

FIG. 6.4. Mic Gobo (Courtesy of ISOVOX)

You can build an isolation booth using movable room gobos.

FIG. 6.5. Isolation Booth Using Movable Room Gobos

Or, if you have the budget, you can buy a prefabricated vocal booth. But make sure it has ventilation, preferably air-conditioning with quiet fans. It can get mighty hot in a non-ventilated tight space.

FIG. 6.6. Prefabricated Vocal Booth (Provided by Whisperroom, Courtesy of Yves Amyot)

When setting up your recording space, also be aware of extraneous noises from air conditioners, HEPA filters, side conversations, etc.

BEFORE YOU HIT THE RECORD BUTTON

What are you listening for when you set up a recording? What sounds good to you? Some recordings need a close, intimate sound with lots of low frequency information in the voice. Some recordings need a distant but powerful sound, with more mid to high frequency information in the voice. How the vocal will sound in the recording is a conversation within the Magic Triangle. Capturing that desired sound begins with selecting the best microphone for the task at hand.

Selecting a Microphone

Choosing the right vocal microphone for your recording is important. The frequency response of a microphone explains how it captures sound across the frequency spectrum. You can find a microphone's frequency response listed in its specifications, usually presented as a line graph, but the best way to select a microphone is to listen to it in action. The frequency response of each microphone can vary enough to reveal subtle timbral differences in a vocal performance.

There are many types of microphones for different applications and instruments, although most vocal recording is done using three types:

1. condenser
2. dynamic
3. ribbon

Condenser microphones are considered as excellent recording mics because of their ability to capture a wide frequency response. Condensers use a charged capacitor plate and a moving element plate, acting as a diaphragm, which transfers the fluctuations of air from your voice into electrical voltages that have a low output. The capacitor can be charged by an induction of phantom power (standardized at 48 volts but also available as 12 or 24 volts in older systems), or a proprietary power supply provided by the manufacturer. This output is then raised in level using a *mic preamp*. Because of their high sensitivity, they capture more timbral detail than dynamic microphones, meaning you will hear clearer highs and lows than with most other microphone types. For this reason, your vocal may need less EQ. Note that because a condenser is more fragile than a dynamic microphone, you might want to use it exclusively in the studio.

Dynamic microphones are the most common choice in live performances, because of their robust construction. Like condensers, they transfer fluctuations of air from your voice into electrical voltages; however, they do this by moving a (copper) coil fixed within the magnetic field of a permanent magnet, which is attached to a fluctuating diaphragm. A mic preamp is also required to raise a dynamic mic's output level for optimum recording, though phantom power is not necessary. Dynamic mics tend to pick up slightly less detail in upper frequencies, so they may sound "darker" than condensers. This is not a concern when you understand how to use EQ and compression effectively.

Ribbon microphones work similarly to dynamic microphones except that they use a thin corrugated metal ribbon suspended inside the magnetic field instead of a copper coil. The ribbon responds to air velocity instead of sound pressure because of its low mass. Since both sides of the ribbon move identically, ribbon microphones are bidirectional. This means that both sides pick up sound equivalently. When you have one vocalist, the other side will likely pick up some room sound. Two vocalists can share this mic by facing each other. A good ribbon microphone can have a much more sensitive frequency response than a dynamic microphone, which can place it as a viable competitor to condensers in a mic shootout.

Both condenser and ribbon microphones use phantom power. Note that it's important to connect them to the preamp *before* you turn on phantom power, to avoid damaging them.

Mic "Shootout"

If you are trying to decide between a few different microphones, you can do a "mic shootout" to compare how they sound. Mic shootouts are very useful when you're buying a microphone, or when you're evaluating the best mic choice for a vocalist you've never recorded before. (If you only have one microphone, ask your local music store about mic rentals and/or their return policy, in order to select a few to evaluate.)

To do a mic shootout, aim all the microphones at a center point around the vocalist's face, regardless of the type of mics you're choosing between. The purpose of this is to gauge variations in the exact same performance with a single microphone. You might need the vocalist to back off 6 to 12 inches so that each mic gets an equivalent signal. You are listening for how the voice sounds on each mic, and how it fits with the composition you're working on. This is a tricky thing to gauge because there are many factors at play (the instrumentation, the density of the arrangement, the range that the vocalist is singing in, the projection of the performance, etc.). Listening for good articulation and a sound that is not too dull or too bright are good places to begin your microphone evaluation. As you compare more microphones, you will begin to discern their differences.

FIG. 6.7. Mic Shootout

Why the Microphone's Polar Pattern Matters

Microphones can have a variety of sensitivity patterns, based on what you're trying to pick up from the vocalist. The *on-axis point* is the position that optimizes the capture and translation of sound for all microphones. This point can also be envisioned as a vertical or horizontal pole, which is surrounded by a space, called the "polar pattern."

Each of the following polar patterns indicates optimal on-axis positioning as you address the microphone. Let's explore the most common polar patterns. (These patterns are usually indicated by the manufacturer on your microphone(s).)

- *Cardioid.* A heart-shaped pressure gradient pattern with a single on-axis point, at the top of a front address mic. Or, at a perpendicular angle of a side address mic. Zero degrees (0°) is the on-axis point that delivers the optimum vocal sound. Note in figure 6.8 that the back of the cardioid pattern has the least sensitivity response. One *front address* mic example is the classic Shure SM-58. One *side address* mic example is the AKG 414, which has three selectable patterns.

a. b.

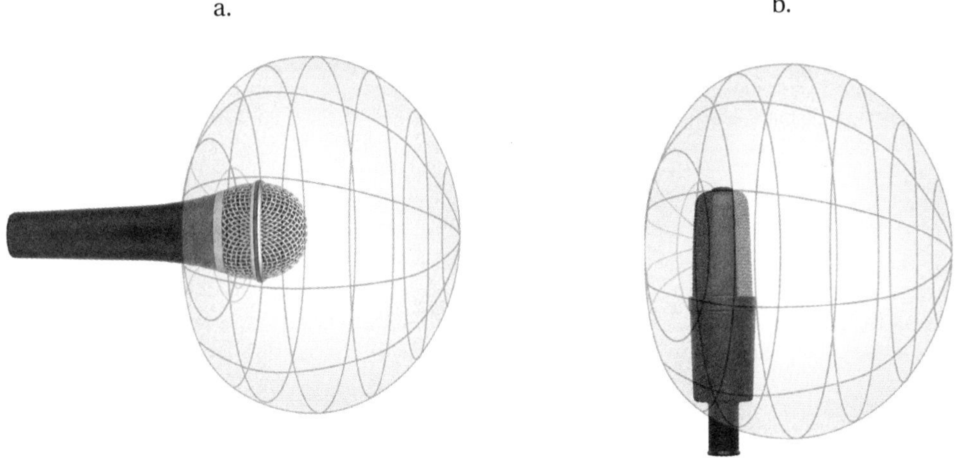

FIG. 6.8. Dynamic Cardioid Polar Pattern, (a) Front Address, (b) Side Address

- *Bidirectional.* A figure-8 shaped gradient pattern with two on-axis points, front and rear, at a perpendicular angle. The on-axis points are at 0° and 180°. Note in figure 6.9 that there is a minimal sensitivity response in between the two polar axes. A bidirectional pattern can be selected from a mic with multiple pattern options, such as the Neumann U-87 and the AKG 414.

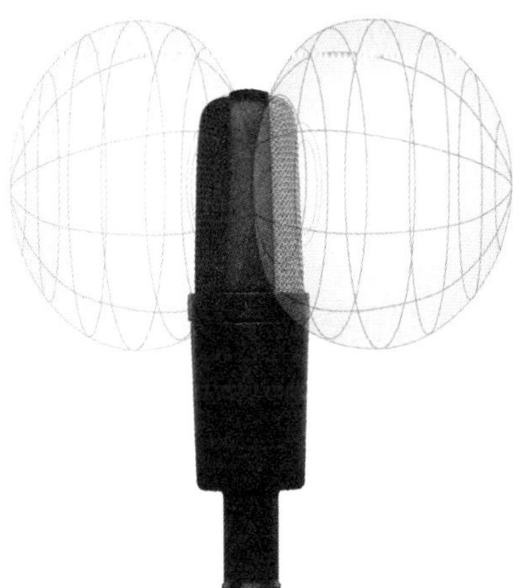

FIG. 6.9. Condenser Bidirectional Polar Pattern, Double Side Address

- *Omnidirectional.* A circular, pressure-sensitive pattern that is equally responsive at any point around a side address or a front address microphone. Note in the picture that there is no specific axis, and some lower end proximity information (a plosive sound that makes b's and p's pop) will not be captured. An omnidirectional pattern can also be selected from a mic with multiple pattern options.

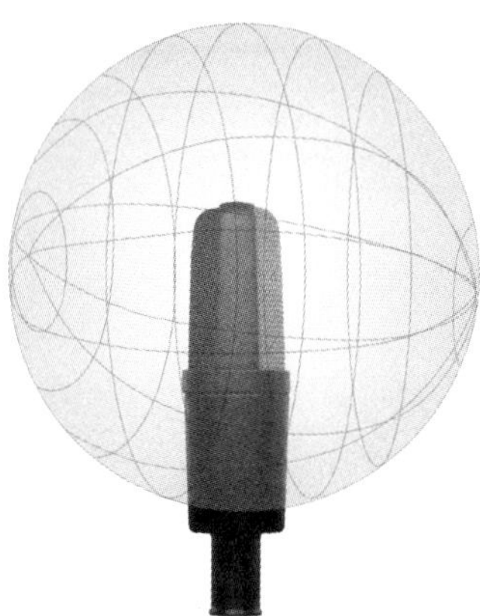

FIG. 6.10. Condenser Omnidirectional Polar Pattern

Bidirectional-only and omnidirectional-only microphones are available, though more often you will use a multi-pattern microphone to select either of those patterns, when recording vocals in the studio.

How do these patterns affect your recording? A *cardioid* pattern will pick up sounds primarily from one side, so if you are trying to focus the recording on a singer and exclude the room sound, that pattern is usually preferred. An *omnidirectional* pattern will pick up sounds from all directions, which is useful if you want to capture a room sound, or are recording a group of people surrounding the microphone on all sides. A multiple-pattern microphone is more versatile than a single-pattern microphone and is a great purchase as your vocal production techniques mature.

Vocalist's Position in the Room

Where the vocalist stands (or sits) in a room can affect how well their voice is captured on the microphone. Reflective surfaces (such as wood walls, concrete floors, glass windows, etc.) will impact the sound of a recorded vocal, so it's best to select a position for the vocalist that minimizes those reflections. If you can't avoid reflective surfaces, you can pad them with soft materials such as blankets, rugs, and foam squares, or you can use gobos.

Great communication in the session includes the ability for everyone to see one another, called the *sight line.*

- **Direct sight line.** The best sight line option is when the vocalist and producer can see each other. In some larger commercial studios, there is a control room and recording room with a window that provides a direct sight line. An even more intimate setup is to move the vocalist into the control room with the producer. The reflections within a large studio control room are usually managed well, so this shouldn't pose a problem. In a smaller environment with a lower budget, the artist and producer will often work in the same room, which offers a great sight line and quick communication.

- **No sight line.** Without a sight line, a vocal session can really slow down, because all communication between the vocalist and the producer will be verbal. Head nodding, moving away from the microphone, winking, smiling, and other non-verbal clues cannot be used. Even something as simple as counting off a section can't happen visually without a direct sight line.
- **Video sight line.** Some recording facilities employ a video system if there is no direct sight line. Minimally, the producer will have a monitor and will watch the singer for any relevant non-verbal clues. A two-way monitoring system, where the producer can see the singer and the singer can see the producer is preferable, but be wary that the video monitor near the microphone is well grounded, lest you introduce grounding noise into your vocal recording.
- **Self-recording.** When you are self-recording at home, to maximize your sound proofing, you might need to move into a different area than the transport controls of your DAW. If so, you can trigger your DAW remotely with a controller app, or set up record-in and record-out points.

Also keep in mind to stay in constant communication with the vocalist, whether directly or through their headphone mix. If they can see you but not hear you, the vocalist might feel excluded from the production process.

Music Stand

A music stand is often needed for lyrics, sheet music, and arrangement charts. Performance notes such as where to breathe, syllables to accent, new ad-libs, etc. can be jotted down on paper or typed into a cell phone, and placed on the music stand for easy reference. (Be sure the phone's ring and vibrate functions are off.) An effective producer works with the vocalist from a copy of the same notes. Keep in mind that music stands are reflective surfaces, and have the potential to add unwanted ambiance to the recorded vocal. An engineer or self-producer can identify problems, such as unwanted reflections, by soloing the voice during the playback of a recording. Make sure to train your ears to hear reflections and other sounds that detract from a well-recorded vocal.

WORKING WITH THE DAW

As mentioned, a DAW is a software application used to record, edit, and produce audio. Within your DAW are tools called "plug-ins" that allow you to modify sounds that you record, and sounds that you play back. Some of the modifications that can be made are "destructive," meaning they cannot be undone. Some are non-destructive, meaning they can be changed at some other time, or undone.

A few of the most important aspects of focus for the recordist (audio engineer) should be input levels, level management, and EQ. These elements all work together to create the vocal recording needed for your song.

Input Levels and Level Management

The meters on your DAW's recording track can help you to understand how much input (recording) level is captured on that track. To make this simple, too much input level will distort the vocal recording on the track, which is usually undesirable. The unit of measurement for amplitude (level) in digital systems is dBFS (*decibels relative to full scale*), which have a defined maximum peak of 0.

Most DAWs have color-coded indicators that can give you an idea of what is a good recording level and what is a poor recording level. In figure 6.11, the numbers on the right indicate the input level in dBFS of the audio signal coming into each channel (what you are recording). The numbers on the left represent each channel's playback level (what you hear) that can be raised or lowered with the virtual fader. Looking left to right in figure 6.11, the first input-level range shown is -30 to -40 dBFS, which is too low for a good quality vocal signal. The second range is -30 to -8 dBFS, which is much better for vocals and should yield a good, clear recording. The third range is -8 to 0 dBFS, which could introduce distortion into your recording when level peaks created by fast transients (such as the consonants "t" and "p") are captured—even though the meter won't show a (red) warning indicator. The fourth range is above the optimum recording level, and *will* distort your recording and show a warning indicator, which is usually red.

a. b. c. d.

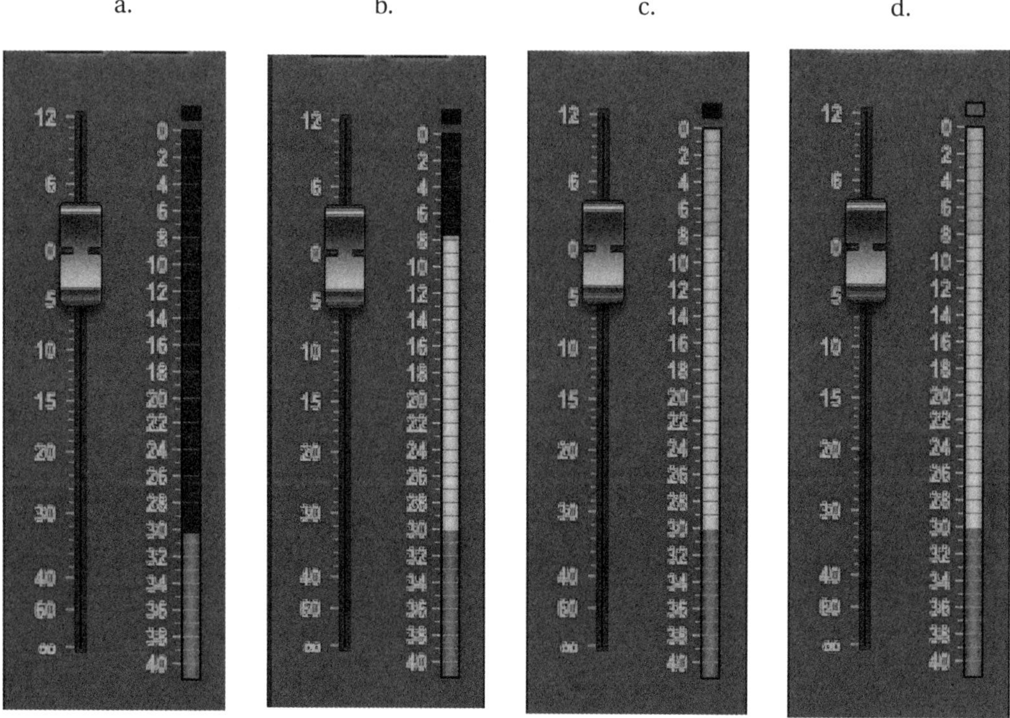

FIG. 6.11. Vocal Levels: (a) too low, (b) good, (c) a bit more than necessary, (d) too strong

Equalization (EQ)

To EQ or not to EQ? EQ (equalization) raises or lowers the frequency response of a recorded vocal performance around a center frequency. A good microphone choice, coupled with good microphone and vocal technique, can mitigate the need for recording with EQ.

But if your vocal is too dark or dull sounding, or it is too bright and sibilant sounding, you can use EQ on the monitoring path of the vocal track. This insertion point for the EQ will not be recorded, but will help the vocal to sound more in line with what is needed for the song.

The standard professional application of EQ and dynamics-processing units is "in series" or "serial," meaning they are placed on the insert of the audio channel in your DAW.

As you add more devices, the audio signal moves through them in sequential order.

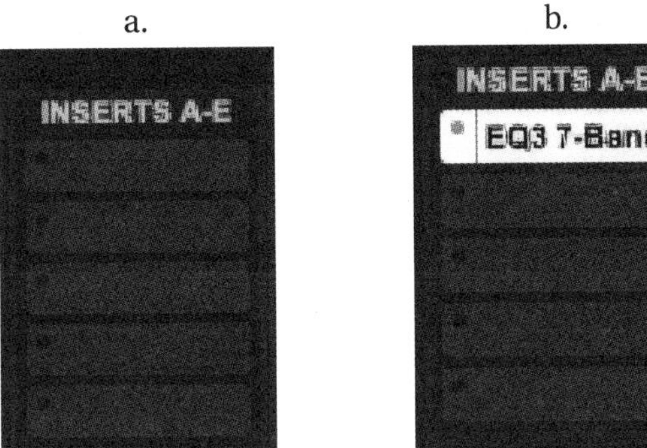

FIG. 6.12. Vocal Playback Track Insertion Section: (a) without EQ, (b) with EQ: you would click on the EQ button to see the frequencies to be adjusted

In our example, the "EQ3 7-Band" button, which has been placed on the insert of an audio track, opens a window that provides access to a high pass filter, seven bands of EQ, and a low pass filter. Figures 6.13 through 6.16 show zoomed-in portions of the filters and the adjustable bands.

Some frequencies for vocal recording that you want to review are:

- 60 Hz and below are commonly rolled off with a *high-pass filter* to eliminate popping p's, popping b's, and floor rumble.

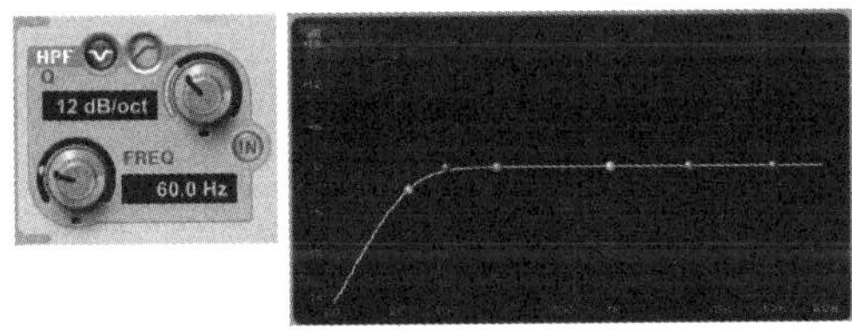

FIG. 6.13. A 60 Hz High Pass Filter Roll-Off

- 200 Hz can be used to add a bit more body to a vocal but might also make a vocal sound dark or dull. A slight boost for thin-sounding vocals or a slight attenuation for dull sounding vocals can be useful in this frequency range.

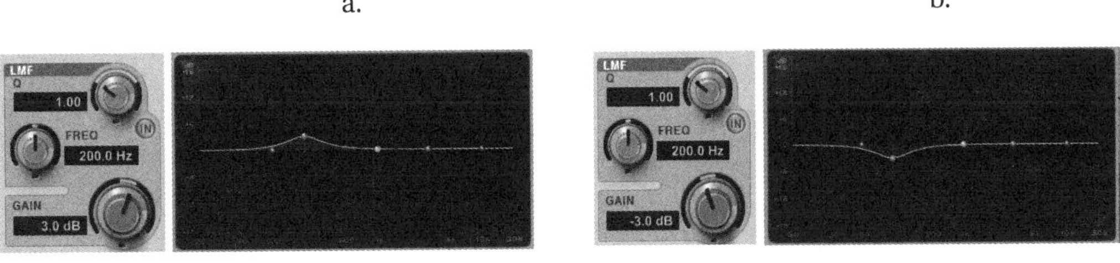

FIG. 6.14. Hz Boost or Attenuation: (a) a slight 200 Hz boost for a thin vocal, (b) a slight 200 Hz attenuation for a dull vocal

- 1 to 5 kHz can be used to add a bit more clarity and articulation to a vocal but might also make a vocal sound too harsh or bright. A slight boost for a vocal that needs more clarity or a slight attenuation for a vocal that is hurting your ears (harsh) can be useful in this frequency range.

a. b.

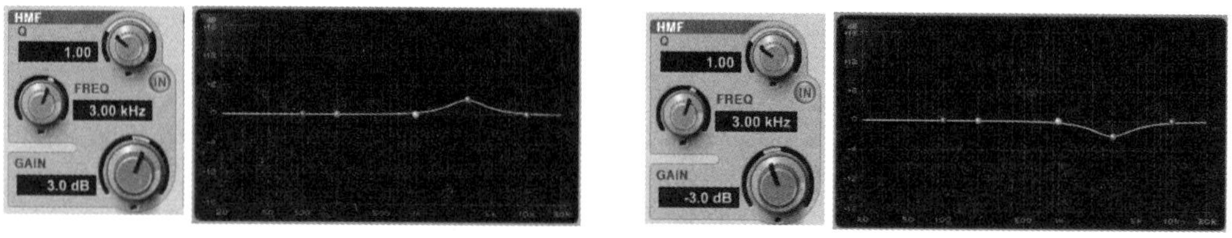

FIG. 6.15. 3 kHz Boost or Attenuation: (a) a slight 3 kHz boost for more vocal clarity, (b) a slight 3 kHz attenuation for a harsh vocal

- 10 to 14 kHz can be added for vocal presence and "sizzle" but might also make a vocal more sibilant. (Sibilance is a hissing sound that occurs when there is too much high frequency energy, most often when articulating the letter "s.") A boost for a vocal that needs more presence, or attenuation for a vocal that is aggressive in the higher frequencies, can be useful in this frequency range.

a. b.

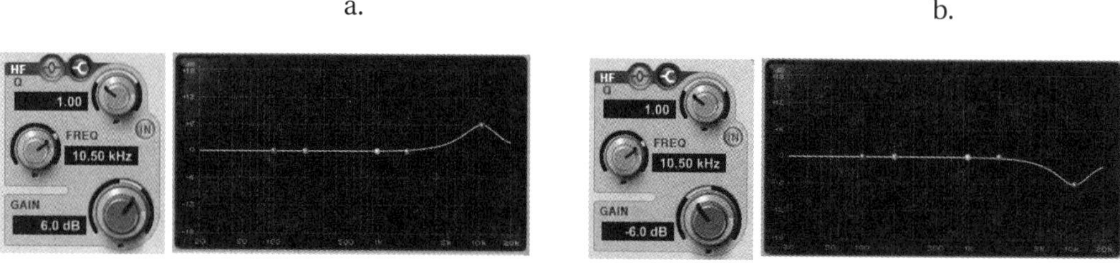

FIG. 6.16. 10 to 14 kHz Boost or Attenuation: (a) a 10 to 14 kHz boost for more vocal presence, (b) a 10 to 14 kHz attenuation for a vocal that is aggressive in the higher frequencies

Compression

Compression is one of the most misunderstood audio processing devices in the recording industry. Compression is attenuation—meaning, it turns sound down. When a vocalist performs on the mic and reaches a loud passage, for example, you might want to turn that moment down so that it doesn't stick out too much. You can use a fader to turn it down manually, but a compressor does it for you automatically. When you are lowering the signal, either manually or with a compressor, you are narrowing the dynamic range between the loud performance and the soft performance. This dynamic processing is used in all genres, but for some genres such as pop, it used heavily to flatten dynamic ranges. For other genres, such as jazz or classical music, it is used more mildly to manage periodic moments in the performance that are too loud.

A typical compressor usually has input, output, ratio, threshold, attack, release, hold, gain reduction (lowering the output), and "make up" gain control (raising or lowering the overall output). You can place a compressor across the insert section of your recording track, similar to the way that you insert EQ on that track. Remember, the standard practice is to add the compressor in series *after* the EQ, so the compressor manages both the incoming vocal signal as well as the added EQ. This helps the vocal to stand out in a recording. Note that these inserts are only affecting the *playback* of the performance. They are not being recorded onto the vocal track. The vocal is being recorded untreated, but you're monitoring processing that can be adjusted later on, as desired.

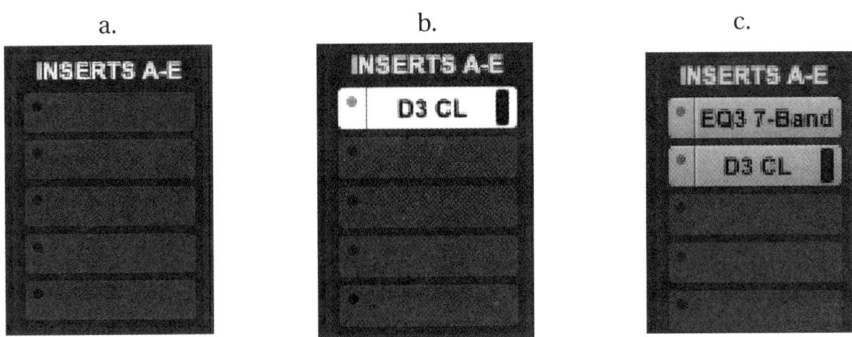

FIG. 6.17. Vocal Playback Track's Insertion Section: (a) with no plug-ins, (b) with a compressor, (c) with an EQ and a compressor in series (meaning one feeds the other)

The "D3 CL" button opens a window with controls for a compression ratio potentiometer ("pot"), a threshold meter, an input-output meter, and a gain reduction (GR) meter, that are shown in figure 6.18. Figure 6.18 displays these parameters when there is no compression in use. The meter on the right (c) shows an input signal of -10 dB, and an output signal of -10 dB. This means that no compression is being applied. That is reflected in the middle picture (b), where the straight vertical line is the threshold at -20 dB, and nothing is being attenuated. The diagonal line is the amplitude (strength) of the incoming signal, moving from left to right. The ratio window on the left (a) is at 1:1, meaning it is not active.

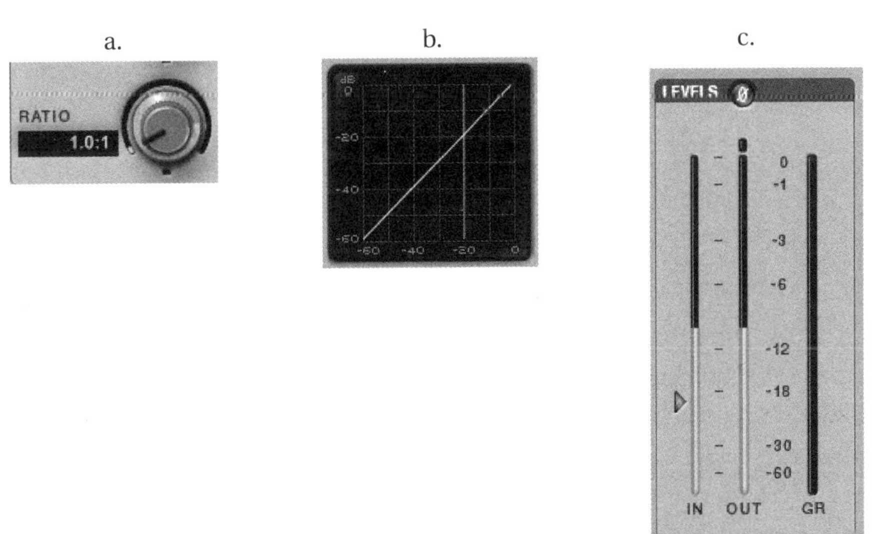

FIG. 6.18. A Non-Compressed Signal: (a) no compression (1:1 ratio), (b) with a –20 dB threshold (vertical line), (c) a –10 dB input signal yielding a –10 dB output

Figure 6.19 shows you what a compressed signal looks like. The gain reduction shown here is the most gain reduction you might use to achieve a subtle use of compression, which is a good place to begin when you are new to compressors. The plug-in on the right (c) shows an input signal of -10 dB and an output signal of -17.5 dB. This means that a transparent amount of compression is being applied, which is reflected in the middle picture, showing a straight vertical line set at the threshold point of -20 dB. This attenuates any output signal above that point (-20 dB). The diagonal line (b), moving from left to right, is bending at this threshold point. The ratio window in the left picture (a) is set at 4:1. This means that for every 4 dB of output *over* the threshold, only 1 dB will be actually be output. As soon as the signal goes above -20, it begins to be compressed (attenuated). If the signal rises 4 dB above -20 (-16 dB), it will only output 1 dB more, which is -19 dB. If the signal rises 8 dB above -20 dB (-12 dB), it will only output 2 dB more, which is -18 dB. Finally, if the signal rises 10 dB above -20 dB (-10 dB), it will only output 2.5 dB more, which is -17.5 dB, as shown in figure 6.19c. The net result is the compressor won't let the signal reach -10 dB. So, what is coming in is -10, but what is going out is -20 + 2.5, or -17.5 (which is 7.5 dB quieter than -10 dB).

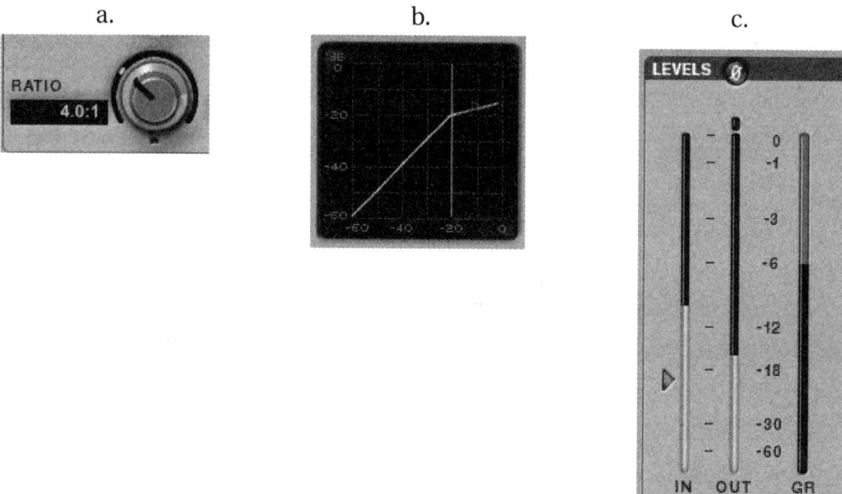

FIG. 6.19. Compression Example (a) a 4:1 ratio, (b) with a –20 dB threshold (vertical line), (c) a –10 dB input signal yielding a –17.5 dB output

The attack, release, hold, and make-up parameters are not standard on all compressors. The attack setting controls how long the compressor takes to compress the signal, while the release setting controls how long the compressor takes to return to 0. The hold setting controls how long the signal remains in a compressed state, after the signal drops below the threshold, before it is released. Because compression turns audio levels down, the make-up gain is used to bring the volume levels back to pre-compression levels within the song.

Note that some compressors change the make-up gain control *automatically* the more you compress—in effect, turning down the peaks (loudest moments), yet raising the output level of the entire performance. This is one reason why compression can be so confusing! Almost all vocal recordings use compression to some degree, and because it can be difficult to listen to songs for examples of how much compression to use, you'll need to experiment with it on your own. When used minimally (no more than -3 to -6 dB of gain reduction), along with good microphone technique, compression can help the vocal stand out in your recording.

If you are advised to purchase an *outboard* (physically separate) microphone preamp, keep in mind that many models contain compressors, which could lead to printing compression on the vocal performance that can't be undone. Printing compression should only be done once you have gained sufficient experience with dynamic processing. Until then, if you are set on using an outboard compressor, it should be used minimally when recording.

Reverb

Reverb gives a sense of the space that the vocal tracks will occupy in the song. Without reverb, the vocal can sound solitary and unconnected to other instruments in the song. With reverb, the vocal sounds more connected to the other instruments, and *spatially* interesting. Reverb is usually helpful during recording for the vocalist who is listening to their performance through headphones, for the producer who is critiquing through studio speakers, and for the audience to enjoy the final recording.

While the standard professional way to add EQ and compression is in series, the way to add time-based effects (reverb and delay) is in parallel. Using reverb in parallel means that you are sending signal through a *bus* using a *send* from the vocal track. The reverb itself is on a separate and independent auxiliary track that receives its input signal from the bus. Parallel-effects processing, as opposed to in-series or serial-effects processing, is the best way to set up your vocal recording track(s) in your DAW. This technique is efficient because it allows multiple tracks to share one effects processor, therefore reducing overall CPU (computer processor) load.

Figure 6.20 shows a parallel reverb configuration prepared to send the vocal track audio to a parallel auxiliary input track. The auxiliary input track has a reverb unit across its insert set to 100% wet, but no audio is being sent to the mix output yet.

a.

b.

FIG. 6.20. Parallel Reverb Configuration. No signal is being sent to the reverb from Send A. (a) Edit view, (b) Mix view

Figure 6.21 shows the same parallel reverb configuration, sending a -10 dB version of the vocal track to a parallel auxiliary input track. The auxiliary input track has a reverb unit across its insert set to 100% wet. The audio of the vocal track and the auxiliary input track (the reverb) are both being sent to the mix output. The result is a vocal with reverb, and the level of the reverb can be adjusted with the send fader.

a. b.

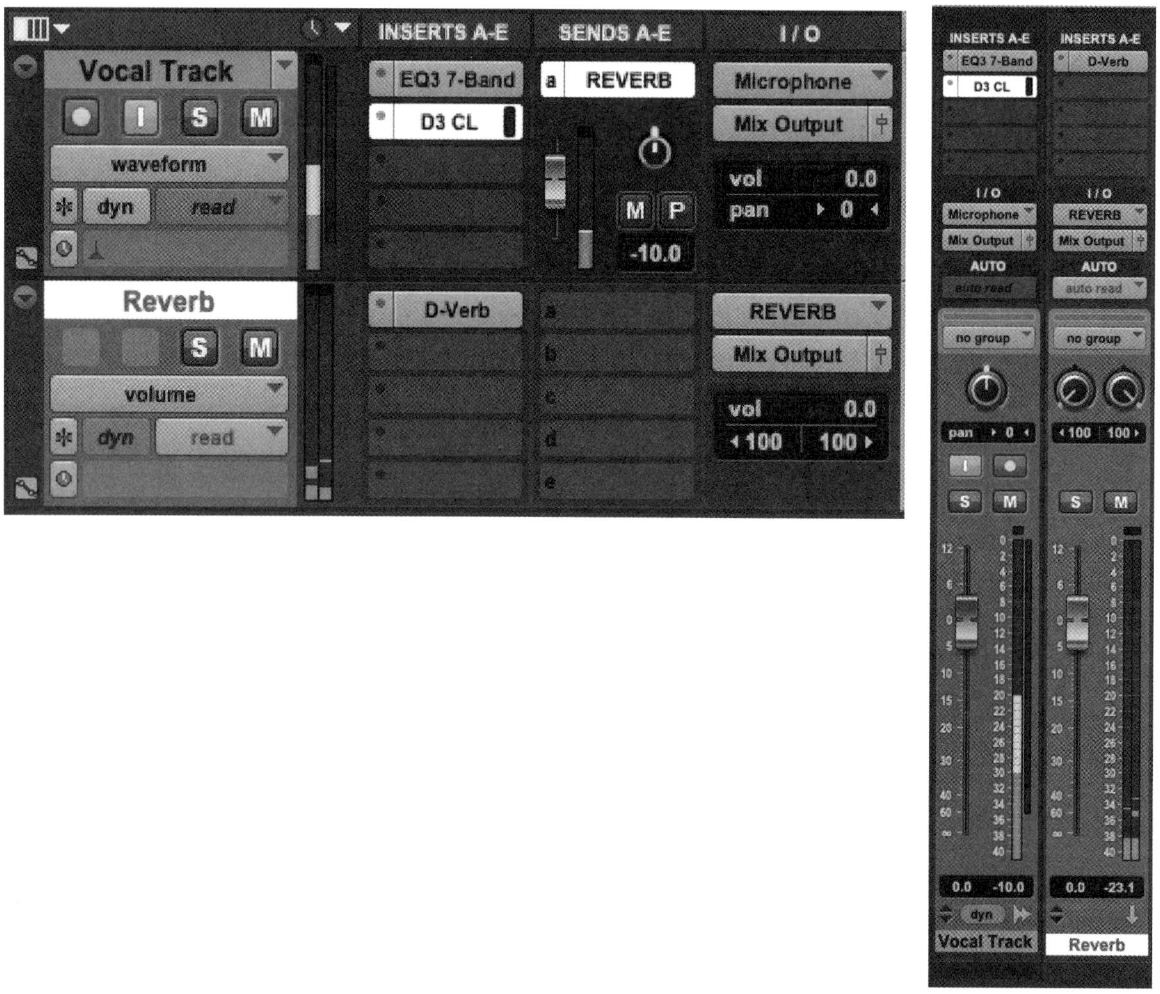

FIG. 6.21. Parallel Reverb Configuration. A –10 dB signal being sent to the reverb from Send A. (a) Edit view, (b) Mix view

When using reverb in parallel, set it to 100 percent *wet*. The level of the send fader determines how much reverb is added to the vocal. In figure 6.22, the reverb example is set to 100 percent wet.

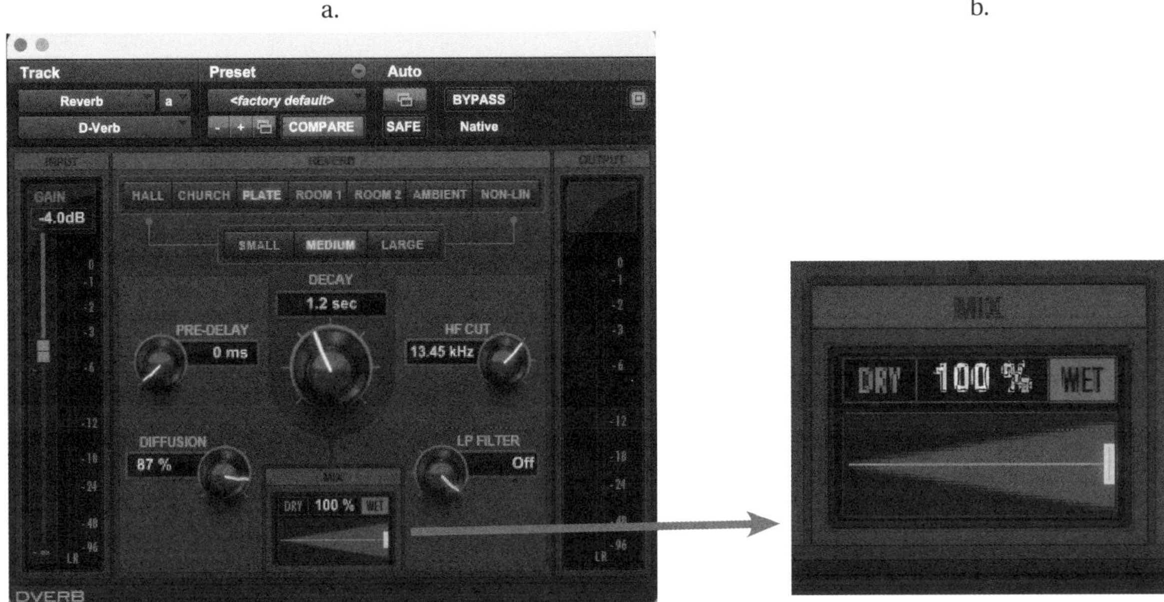

FIG. 6.22. Wet Reverb Setup: (a) reverb set at 100 percent wet, (b) close-up of mix wet/dry ratio setting

Here are a few setting ideas that can be used for your vocal recording setup. The reverb time (decay time) determines how long you hear reverb before it fades. Longer reverbs work well for recording ballads at 60 bpm to 75 bpm. Try using hall and church presets set from 2 to 6 seconds. Medium reverbs work well for mid-tempo compositions at 75 bpm to 100 bpm; plate and larger room presets could be set from 1.2 seconds to 4 seconds. Short reverbs work well for up-tempo and dance compositions, as well as rap vocals, at 100 to 160 bpm. Short room and early reflection presets could be set from 375 ms to 2.5 seconds.

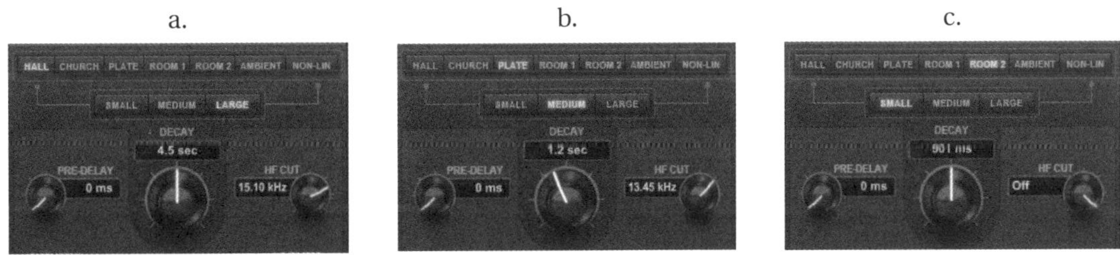

FIG. 6.23. Reverb Settings: (a) long reverb setting, (b) medium reverb setting, (c) short reverb setting

Remember that if you use reverb in series, rather than in parallel, it increases your CPU load. That's because you would need to open up a new reverb plug-in for each new vocal track. When used in series, the reverb unit controls how much reverb is being applied via its wet/dry ratio. Furthermore, when used in series, even a deceivingly low wet/dry ratio like 15 to 20 percent applies more reverb than necessary to the dry signal.

TIP: PREPARE MULTIPLE VOCAL TRACKS IN ADVANCE

A very useful tip for vocal recording is to create multiple vocal recording tracks with identical input, EQ, compression, and reverb sends before you start recording. Having identical settings on each track will speed up the creative process when you are thinking your way through new melodies or creating new harmony parts. Although we have conveniently labeled these tracks for different background vocal parts, any track can be used to double or comp the lead, if needed in the heat of the creative process.

In the figure 6.24 example, each track has its own reverb send fader. Each fader can be adjusted individually for how much reverb you hear—but, they're all sharing the same reverb unit.

FIG. 6.24. Seven Vocal Tracks with EQ, Compression, and Reverb

Song Position and Beat Subdivisions

Before you begin recording, it is important to set the correct tempo of the song in the DAW session. Your DAW's click track provides an audible marker for the downbeats in your composition. All DAWs display bars (measures), beats, and sub-beat positions (ticks) prominently in the project window, which is useful as you record and edit the song. As you play your song, a vertical line showing the current playback position in the tracks area, moves along in real-time across the bar/beat position ruler.

Figure 6.25 shows an example of a bar/beat ruler, with one bar in 4/4 time. In this example, beats 1/1/000 through 2/1/000 are subdivided four times with vertical lines, indicating where quarter notes would occur in your song. The thinner vertical lines indicate where sixteenth notes would occur.

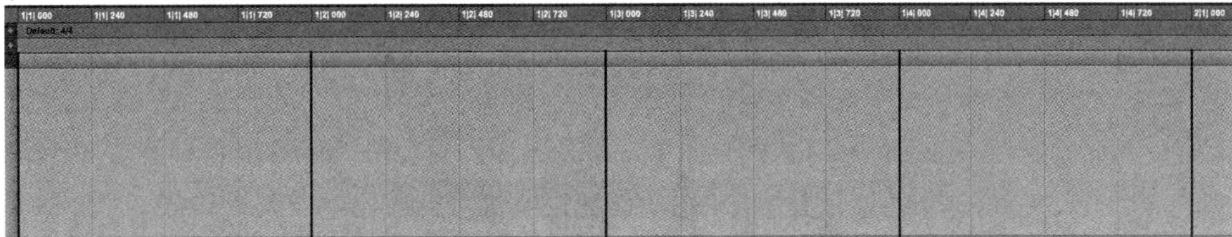

FIG. 6.25. Sub-Beats in a DAW Track Display

Figure 6.26 shows the same positions in music notation. These represent the same beat positions as in figure 6.25.

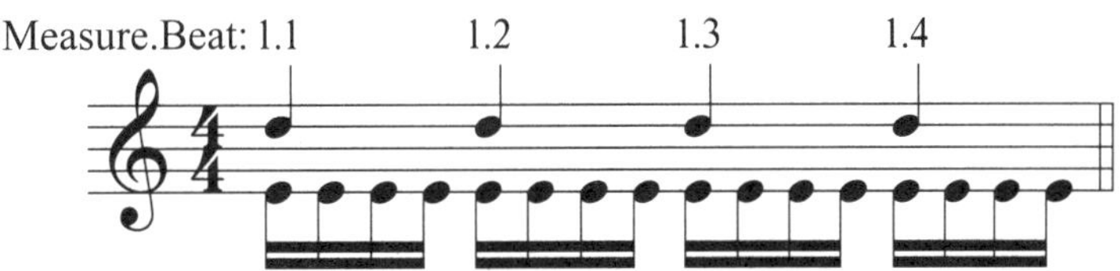

FIG. 6.26. Music Notation Values

Keeping track of each downbeat and subdivision enables accurate pre-rolls and punch-ins. *Pre-rolls* allow you to start the playback a measure or two before the recording bar/beat location. This gives the vocalist a moment to listen as they prepare the physical, emotional, and stylistic aesthetics of their performance. *Punch-ins* are a useful way to fix a segment of a previous recording, by selecting a small area of that performance to rerecord. This is done by choosing an in-point and an out-point for the new recording, which can then be punched in manually by the recordist or automatically using the DAW's auto-record functions.

Your recording precision will be heightened when the team knows the exact locations for the punch-in and punch-out points. For instance, saying something like "Punch in on bar 25 beat 2 for two bars and then punch out" is common for those that use the DAW and music notation to its fullest.

Or, the vocalist could say, "Punch in the first two lines of chorus 1 and then punch out." If the chorus begins on bar 25, you would not start playback on bar 25. You would ask if the artist wants one bar or two bars of pre-roll before the punch. If they said one bar, you would play from bar 24 and then go in to record at bar 25. If they said two bars, you would play from bar 23 and then go in to record at bar 25. This is a huge time saver in recording situations that allow the vocalist to retain their creative choices with a minimum of fumbling for the correct playback point.

Note that some punches are best done by listening to the phrase being rerecorded-rather than using bars and beats. Using this method you select the appropriate words, or breaths, for setting the in and out points.

Another increase of efficiency is to use your DAW's labeling for each section as an intro, verse, chorus, bridge, etc., as in figure 6.27. It is easy to overlook this idea if you are looking at the recorded audio and have an idea of where each section is.

But it is better to be *certain* of where and what each section is than to have *an idea* of where and what each section is—even more so, when you have not seen the song for a few weeks or months.

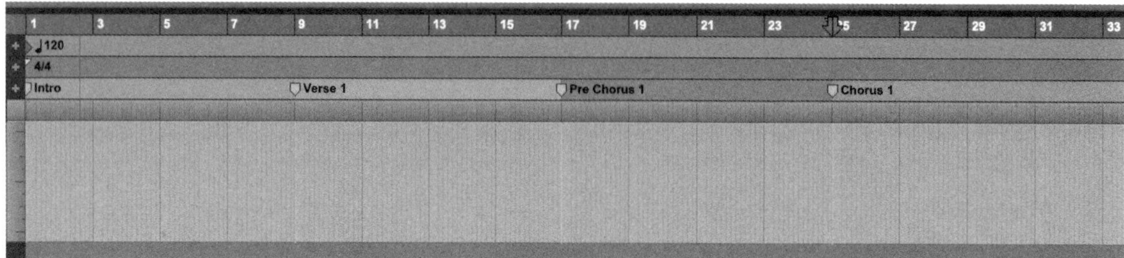

FIG. 6.27. `A 32-Bar Song Arrangement, Showing: Tempo (120), Time Signature (4/4), and Song Sections. (Intro, Verse 1, Prechorus 1, Chorus 1)

Rough Mix

Most vocal recordings in contemporary music are performed against a rough mix. When multiple instrumental tracks of a song are initially mixed down to a two-track version, this two-track version is usually labeled a "rough mix" because it is a rough approximation of what the song will be for the final mix. When the vocalist needs more or less of the rough mix to perform against, the rough mix provides a simple way to raise or lower the entire song.

The drawback is that you cannot isolate, raise, or lower individual parts within the rough mix for the vocalist if they request it. Therefore, when your vocalist is keying off of certain instruments and needs more or less of them, there is an alternative approach. You can route the entire multitracked instrumental composition to a stereo auxiliary fader. In this way you can adjust individual track levels as needed. This approach is almost identical to the two-track version because you can raise or lower the volume of the entire song—while maintaining the ability to isolate, raise and lower any instrument.

Either of these two approaches can work well for quick recording setup time in your vocal session.

CHAPTER 7

Let's Record

GETTING COMFORTABLE WITH HEADPHONES

Before you begin recording, the vocalist should take a bit of time to become comfortable with using headphones. Over-the-ear headphones block out much of the ambient sound. The result is that the vocalist only hears their own voice through the headphones. They are not hearing their voice bouncing around the acoustic space and reaching their ears in a natural way. This can be disconcerting and disorienting for many vocalists, especially the first few times that they record. The more a vocalist records, the more they will get used to feeling isolated. It should eventually feel like a natural part of the recording process.

If this lack of acoustic ambience is truly intolerable for the vocalist—and it does bother even some seasoned pros—a potential remedy is to remove one earpiece from their ear. This raises the likelihood that the headphone will bleed into the vocal recording, yet the pitch accuracy can be worth it for some vocalists. If the off-ear headphone is aimed to the rear of the head, or pulled up slightly from the ear, this can also be helpful. Another option is to pan the entire mix to one side, so that only one earpiece has audio present.

Since headphones are actually small speakers, keeping them secure on the vocalist's ears reduces the chance that the microphone will also capture the headphones output.

Headphones Mix

Getting the right blend of vocal-to-instrumental level is critical. If the vocalist cannot hear themselves or the rough mix well, then their entire performance can suffer. Pitch, timing, attitude, and which vocal register to use can be difficult to fine-tune if heard too softly or too loudly through the headphones. Listen to the headphones mix that the vocalist is listening to in order to gauge their monitoring tastes. To get the initial headphones level, warn the vocalist to start with the headphones somewhat off their ears, in case the music comes on too loudly, at first.

MIC TECHNIQUE

For a vocalist, "mic technique" refers to their relationship with the microphone for the purpose of creating a listenable performance. Generally the vocalist will stay within a consistent distance from the mic, while adjusting their position moderately for louder or softer passages. When done well, this can be considered great mic technique. But when done poorly, it can create an unevenly recorded vocal performance.

It's normal for a vocalist to feel awkward and uncomfortable the first time they hear their voice through a microphone and headphones. That is because singing into a mic for the purposes of making a record is a different aural experience than singing in an acoustic space for a live performance. With practice, the vocalist will recognize their vocal sound, and how they can use mic technique to create a wide range of vocal qualities within their recordings. The vocalist's job is not only to perform, but also to interact with the microphone. For the duration of the vocal session, the vocalist will have a relationship with the microphone, whether as a self-producer or as part of a production team.

Think of singing into a microphone for a recording as if it is "filmmaking," and singing into an acoustic space for maximum projection as if it is "the Broadway stage." In filmmaking, the actor's face can take up the entire screen, while on Broadway, you might need binoculars to see the actor's facial expressions.

For a recordist, "mic technique" simply refers to the placement of the microphone, to optimize amplitude and frequency response. It gets more complex when more than one microphone is in use, such as when recording a choir or a group of vocalists.

For choirs and groups, the recordist can use more than one microphone to capture the full ambient sound. Advanced techniques such as XY, Blumlein, ORTF, Faulkner, M-S, Binaural, spaced Omnis, and Decca tree can be utilized. For a detailed explanation of these microphone techniques, please refer to the publication *Hip-Hop Production: Inside the Beats* by Prince Charles Alexander (Berklee Press).

Distance from the Mic

There are general guidelines for distance from the mic, though each vocalist and production team will need to discover their own best practices. The first thing the vocalist does with the microphone is to find their "spot"—their best standing or sitting distance from the microphone. It's best to place the microphone on a mic stand so that the vocalist does not have to touch it, which would introduce clicks, clacks, rumbles, and other unwanted noises.

A good rule of thumb is for the vocalist's mouth to be positioned 3 to 6 inches away from the microphone for an intimate vocal performance, and no more than 12 to 24 inches away for projected, or belting performance—depending on the microphone being used, and its gain level at the mic preamp. In addition, compressors can be used to help manage level, but using them minimally is best when establishing a new work flow.

At 3 to 6 inches, reflections in the room are minimized and the vocal signal is maximized. This distance is optimum for the lowest notes in a vocalist's range that might be sung in the verse sections of a song. Reference Billie Eilish's entry lines to the verses of "Everything I Wanted" (2019). That level of intimacy, capturing the slightest amount of air, or fry, in the vocal performance, is the result of a close distance to the microphone.

FIG. 7.1. Microphone Proximity. Singing 6 inches from the on-axis point of the microphone.

You can also hear this level of intimacy on Shawn Mendes' verse in "Wonder" (2020). Shawn maintains that airy quality throughout most of the composition with a relatively high mic gain level. But by the time he hits the last line of prechorus 1, and all through chorus 1, he is maximizing his projection, and a 3 to 6 inch distance would likely have resulted in a distorted recording. For those sections, a lower mic gain level was used so his vocal wouldn't distort when he sang more loudly.

Some vocalists who have well-learned mic technique may prefer instead to sing a song all the way through, using their distance from the mic for level management. As you are moving from 3 inches to 12 inches from the on-axis point of the microphone, is that a step back, a lean back or a turn away from the microphone? Congratulations, you have arrived at a critical point of awareness. A vocalist needs a bit of "distance choreography" in order to achieve a good balance for different projection amplitudes.

Sound Check

Once you've made your mic choice and have spoken with your vocalist concerning the approach to the project, the actual work of creating a viable recording begins. The vocalist moves in front of the on-axis point of the microphone, places the headphones on their ear(s), and sound checks their optimal distance for capturing the best vocal signal. The producer should be watching and engaged with this process. This moment is an essential part of capturing a great sound because some changes might need to take place. The microphone pre-amp levels or the vocalist's distance might need to change in order to get the vocal timbre and volume you want. For example, the verse might be breathy and intimate, while the chorus is powerful and belted, as in Olivia Rodrigo's song "Vampire" (2023). If the belted vocal is performed with the breathy mic settings, it could distort and make the recording unusable.

Pop Filter: Peter Piper and the Proximity Effect

Let's do a quick exercise. Place the palm of your hand about two inches away from your mouth and say the phrase, "Peter Piper picked a peck of pickled peppers." Did you feel the air hit your hand during the "P" syllables? If you did, you have just felt the same pressure that will be introduced to your microphone when you say "P" and "B" syllables. These bursts of air pressure can create audible pops or low rumbling sounds in the recording.

Pop and rumble sounds are an exaggeration of the *proximity effect*—where the mic favors low frequencies that are positioned close to the sound source. When used well, it can make the vocal sound more intimate. When pushed to an extreme, you will get the unwanted pops and rumbles.

One way for a vocalist to eliminate pops and rumbles is to move their head back from the mic, or turn their head to the side, pointing away from the on-axis point of the mic. Another way is to pronounce the same phrase with softer "P"s and "B"s.

You've probably seen great vocalists manage their distance from the mic during live performances. When using a hand-held mic, they will move it towards and away from their mouths, creating the necessary distances for a well-captured vocal. This same approach can be used when recording, but instead, your vocalist moves their head or body for the desired distances from the mic stand.

A simple way to manage pops and rumbles is to use a "pop" filter, such as a windscreen or a sponge. The recordist could also use a hi-pass filter on an equalizer, set to about 100 or 150 Hz to eliminate the frequency range where pops and rumbles exist. Body movements, head movements, pop filters and equalizer filters are all viable choices to incorporate once you hear plosives in your recording work.

a.

b.

c.

d.

FIG. 7.2. Pop Filters: (a) pop filter, (b) pop filter in use, (c) sponge, (d) sponge in use

55

In track 55, you'll hear:

1. the "Peter Piper" phrase performed with plosives
2. the phrase performed without plosives

3. the plosives in the first phrase softened with a 130 Hz high pass filter at 12 dB per octave

At this point, the vocalist should be engaged in the performance of the song and not have to deal with technical logistic, so producers and recordists should make sure any technical changes are as non-invasive as possible for the creative flow of the recording session.

Sibilance

Sibilance occurs when the consonants "S," "Z," "C," create a hissing sound at the beginning or ending of a word. Some pronunciations of syllables like "tion" and "Sh" also create a hiss. Sibilant consonants are a natural part of speech (in any language), and are necessary to articulate many words. Some people may naturally speak with strong sibilant consonants, and some microphones exaggerate sibilant frequencies. Too much sibilance can create an unpleasant harshness in recorded vocals. As the producer, you can suggest that the vocalist softens their sibilant sounds, and/or use dynamic processing (a "de-esser") to mitigate them. If a de-esser is overused however, the vocalist could sound like they're lisping.

In track 56, you'll hear:

56

1. a phrase performed with sibilance,
2. the phrase performed with less sibilance, and
3. the sibilance lessened using a de-esser in the DAW.

Breathing Sounds While Recording

For performing leads, as well as backgrounds, there can be common issues at the microphone that can amplify the sound of a breath. With headphones on, vocalist(s) may hear their breaths so loudly that it can inhibit their singing. Also, if they inhale at the last moment before starting a note, you will hear them gasp, which also makes it harder for them to start the note cleanly. Last minute inhalations are natural when we speak, but for recording, encourage your vocalist(s) instead to inhale a moment before they sing (or speak) while visualizing the note and while physically readying it in their mouth and throat. Then sing it. Track 57 demonstrates a vocalist gasping upon inhalation when starting a phrase, then singing by the same phrase without gasping.

57

Movement

Moving your head or taking a slight step forward or backward is normal during vocal performance. Watches, earrings, and other types of loose ornamentation can make sound when moved and will be picked up on the microphone. Even the rustling of a vocalist's arms against certain fabrics, such as a leather or vinyl jacket, can create unwanted noise.

You can record sitting or standing, whichever the vocalist prefers. Be careful of body movement when they are seated, though. Those rustling clothes and creaking chairs might come into play and be picked up on the microphone.

MONITOR MIX

The mix that the recordist and producer will constantly review is called the "monitor mix." In a traditional Magic Triangle setup, the artist is in a recording booth using headphones for monitoring. The recordist and the producer are in a control room using near field, mid field, and/or large monitors for recording and playback.

When the vocalist needs a different perspective on the performance, to check issues that might be difficult to discern under the headphones, it is useful for them to take a break, come into the control room, and review the recording from a different point of view. This builds in breaks and raises awareness about how the vocal performance will translate across different playback systems.

If you are a self-recordist, the same holds true. Come out from under the headphones periodically to review the recording on your speakers. The variance in frequency response can give you more information about your vocal performance's pitch, timing, emotional content, timbre, articulation, and ability to connect to the listener.

CAPTURING THE SCRATCH VOCAL

A *scratch vocal* is a first draft of the lead vocal performance and is commonly how a recording begins. It is used to get into the zone of the recording session while preparing to perform the keeper vocal.

The term "scratch vocal" comes from the process of "scratching," or eliminating, this performance from the final version of the recording.

If a mistake is made on a scratch vocal performance (lyrics forgotten, or slightly off pitch), it is perfectly fine. Keep moving forward to complete the song. Once you are done, go back and fix the forgotten lyric or poorly pitched phrase. There will also be phrases that spill into other phrases awkwardly, but you shouldn't be too concerned, because you can use multiple tracks for the keeper vocal to fix that. You do need to be wary of spending too much time on the scratch vocal process.

The human voice is a fragile instrument, and you want to expend more of the "correcting" energy on the keeper vocal rather than the scratch vocal.

How well prepared are you to capture the vocal performance from take to take? If you are the recordist, speed matters. While the vocalist is warming their voice up, the production team should be getting ready to go, too. That way, as soon as the vocalist is ready to sing and their voice is feeling great, you're also ready for them at that moment.

Remember, when you're setting up, create several tracks at a time for the vocals, not just one—even if there are no supporting background vocals. That way, you can just hop from track to track to do multiple takes, and the vocalist doesn't have to wait for you to set up the next track. (See figure 6.24.)

Now, there are many stories of scratch vocals possessing a magic that could never be replicated by any of the succeeding passes, but the real purpose of the scratch vocal is to set up a guide through the song, sort of like a stand-in actor that goes through the lighting paces on a film before the actual actor is filmed.

Once the scratch vocal is completed, the vocalist and producer should listen to the performance. If the scratch vocal is not providing the necessary guide for the song, now is the time to make changes. You can record new prosody or melodic variations as "punch-ins" that give the song more of what it might need. Once again, be wary of taxing the vocalist, because the human voice is a fragile instrument.

Spend more time correcting the keeper vocal rather than the scratch vocal.

If the composition needs a great deal of structural work, that can be determined and sorted out during the scratch vocal. If that work is substantive, then make the scratch vocal session its own session and leave the keeper session for another day. It will be worth it to your vocalist's voice, and the song will most assuredly also benefit.

When the scratch vocal is providing the necessary guide for the song, it's time to move on to the keeper vocal.

Live Performance Aesthetic

When you are trying to get a live performance aesthetic, the vocalist knows the song. They perform the song all the way through, multiple times, and you pick the best performance, or pieces of the performance, for the final recording.

This approach is suitable for seasoned live performers who can deliver nuanced performances with minimal coaching. Céline Dion is one of the vocalists that comes to mind for this way to record. The approach works for music that highlights live performance as the focal point of the work, such as jazz, folk, bluegrass, musical theater, etc.

Listen to Céline Dion's performance video of "My Heart Will Go On" (from the 2007 DVD *Live In Las Vegas - A New Day*). Notice the close proximity of the microphone and the purposeful head turning as she is performing the composition. Even when she belts, the microphone is not more than 6 inches from her lips.

This performance is a master class of vocal technique that also translates well in recording facility situations. One caveat: what you do not see is that there is probably a very good compressor, like a Teletronix LA-2A, working in conjunction with her vocal performance.

Keeper Vocals

The primary job of the vocal producer is to help the vocalist create the best vocal performance possible. Sometimes, that performance can be more than the vocalist thought they were capable of delivering. Your demeanor and your organization of the session are a part of making excellent execution possible. You create the possibility for the vocalist to find their voice in the song, and for them to feel empowered as they explore. When done well, the intention of the vocal performance can emerge.

There are two primary ways to approach a keeper vocal recording session for popular music. They are both viable because they are both in service of a great vocal performance. They are the linear approach and the sectional approach.

In the *linear approach*, you record (for example) the intro followed by verse 1, followed by prechorus 1, followed by chorus 1, followed by verse 2, followed by prechorus 2, followed by chorus 2 followed by the bridge, followed by chorus 3, followed by the outro, and the end. Each section can be scrutinized for how the emotional content is building tension toward a climax (usually chorus 1), once the tension has been released in the chorus another buildup begins in verse 2 building tension to a climax in chorus 2, which then moves into a compositional release of energy in the bridge before the climactic release of energy in the final chorus that culminates with an ending that is often a closure for the entire experience. (This is merely an example of a compositional structure and is not indicative of all compositions. It is merely a guideline for us to uncover the process of vocal recording and producing that reveals itself in songs the way good writing reveals itself in great novels.)

This linear approach is amazing, but it does have drawbacks. If you spend lots of time perfecting verse 1 (which you should, because these are the first vocal phases that listeners will hear, and they set the mood for whether listeners want to engage with the song), you will then need to refocus the energy for prechorus 1, which might demand a bit more stress on the voice.

These two sections alone could take thirty minutes to an hour, with many short breaks, of recording the same phrases over and over again. Small phrases will be punched in, while timbres and intent will be reimagined. Do not be afraid to look at each line as its own separate recording. Some people prefer to record entire sections as one pass, some people prefer to record a line or two before moving to the next line. This is really a preference that the vocalist and the producer will come to an agreement about as the vocal recording plan unfolds. As the sections are recorded, they are reviewed by the producer and the vocalist as a team.

Think about it: the average live vocal concert performance is usually about 45 to 90 minutes long, and in the linear approach, you are not even up to the second verse but have already engaged your vocalist for 60 minutes.

Once you are satisfied that verse 1 and prechorus 1 are building the song well, your next section would be chorus 1. In chorus 1, let's say you have moved an octave away from verse 1 and are working the vocal projection even harder to deliver the needed emotional content. And this lasts for a half an hour. In this model, you can see that you will arrive at an amazing performance, but the voice is being taxed physically with an extended performance duration that would make completing the song in one day a bit prohibitive.

This is another reason why the scratch vocal is so important. You will review your completed keeper performances and use the scratch vocal to fill in work that still needs to be done. This way, you can review the complete song and approach a second day of recording verse 2, prechorus 2, and chorus 2 with fresh vocal chops. If needed, you can reserve more time for the bridge and final chorus work.

In terms of time, this is a huge drawback, but when you think about the many times that you revisit your DAW work now, the amount of time spent arriving at a desired performance is really not that different.

This entire process speeds up, of course, with excellent preparation, well trained vocal chops, and a less than stressful melody. A proficient vocalist might be able to deliver the composition in a linear fashion within a four to six hour session. But, once again, be wary of exhausting the vocal instrument and shifted vocal timbres due to stressed vocal folds. No work will get done if the vocalist has harmed their voice.

Listen to the linear evolution of Shawn Mendes' "Wonder" (2020) across each section. Does it sound like the same vocal sound in verse 1 that he uses in prechorus 1? Does the last line of prechorus 1 sound like the other three lines in that section? Or does it sound like the full projection of chorus 1? "Wonder" is a perfect example of our second keeper-vocal recording session approach, using sectional recording.

In the *sectional approach*, you will most likely begin with verse 1, similar to the approach that you would use for the linear approach. Remember, while the vocalist is recording, the producer's job is to stay focused on their pitch, timing, emotional content, timbre, dynamics, articulation/enunciation, and their ability to connect with the listener. The vocalist's job is to work within the framework of the instrumentation and production—in a sense, merging with it—so they complement one another and all the elements can be heard.

If your multiple passes and multiple punch-ins are yielding wonderful results, the difference between the linear approach and the sectional approach is which section you will work on next.

In the sectional approach, you will move from like section to like section. Since verse 1 and verse 2 have like emotional content, you would complete verse 1 and then move to verse 2—one section type at a time, as opposed to recording the song in order, as it was written. All the interesting textures that you discovered in verse 1 can now be more easily replicated as continuous performance through verse 2. Once these two similar sections have been completed, perhaps the bridge benefits from a similar vocal execution. How do you know this? Aha, the scratch vocal told you so much. It revealed that verse 1, verse 2, and the bridge can use a similar vocal execution and intent. Prechorus 1 and prechorus 2 are also similar sections and can be performed once you have completed the previous verse and bridge work. Once the prechoruses have been completed, you can focus on full projection across choruses 1, 2, and 3.

This approach allows the voice to warm up and become comfortable in a performance state that is consistent for an amount of time. (Breaks for vocalists should be somewhere between 15 and 30 minutes.) It allows the vocalist to preserve discovered nuances from section to section that are a hallmark of popular vocal recording. Once again, reference the similarity of like sections in Shawn Mendes's "Wonder."

The sectional approach is extremely efficient and time effective. It is probably the most common vocal recording approach for popular music.

Drawbacks can be that the amount of time spent on the chorus work, if it is done in the same day, could really stress the vocal cords. If your work plan looks like that is a possibility, the best solution is to move the chorus work to another day and make sure the warmup work is diligent.

Another drawback is that you have to be more deliberate in planning/creating emotional growth between sections. Perhaps you want prechorus 2 to sound slightly more urgent than prechorus 1, but because you are not recording the sections in order, you don't know where the emotional peak of chorus 1 will leave off. Once again, the scratch vocal comes to the rescue to help give you a better idea of how to resolve this issue. Although you might get a slightly different emotional content from the keeper vocal of chorus 1, the scratch vocal of chorus 1 can definitely lead you in the right direction.

Note: Choruses are usually not the first thing sung in a sectional approach. But if the chorus is technically challenging, that could be an option because you have already recorded a scratch vocal.

These examples should give you an idea of how critical the scratch vocal work is in both the sectional and the linear approaches of the keeper vocal. Listen to track 58 to hear a chorus sung as a rough scratch vocal recorded in one pass; then, the chorus
58 is performed again and modified with several punch-ins, to achieve the keeper vocal.

EFFECTIVE USE OF VARYING VOCAL TIMBRES

Of all the vocal execution points that you can focus on, one that gets missed by many vocalists and vocal producers is an effective use of varying timbres. You can have a good melody, with good prosody, but if the vocal timbre lacks variation, the vocal performance can sound stagnant and boring.

Your job as a vocal producer is to be aware of how the subtle nuances of vocal execution can help a vocal performance be the best that it can be for the song. To achieve this, create a simple language between you and your vocalist that communicates different timbral choices. This is how to begin reshaping a bland performance. Use simple words such as "airy," "clear," and "nasal" to get the conversation started. Then, once you hear the range of what the vocalist can give you, keep honing in on defining their timbral palette. There are several artist examples of how timbres can bring out a vocal performance in chapter 4.

SELF-RECORDING STRATEGY

If you are a self-recording vocalist, and you are not sure how to achieve variation in your vocal performance, here's a strategy you could try.

Record three vocal passes.

1. Sing the first pass from top to bottom using only your breathy tone.
2. Sing the second pass from top to bottom using only your chest tone.
3. Sing the third pass from top to bottom using only your mix-to-belt tone.

Then, edit the phrases so that you move from a breathy line to a chest line to a mix-to-belt line to a chest line to a breathy line. You are basically creating an arc that begins small, has a climax in the middle, and then ends small. Do that for phrases, do that for sections, and create a whole song using this arc concept.

Listen to how the intention and emotion are affecting the song using this approach. The goal is to re-sing it with the intentions that you have created from your pre-vocal "Frankenstein" performances.

This is a good way to stir the juices and create options that will push your vocal performance beyond its comfort zone, and to get the most expressive performance possible.

CHAPTER 8

Comping and Editing Your Recorded Vocal Performance

COMPING

When you are recording a vocal, anything short of perfection can be a reason to perform the vocal phrases again, and again, and again. Fortunately, because of multitrack recording, there are other options available. In contemporary popular recording, *comping* (creating a single compilation of the best pieces from several performances) is the usual approach to getting a great vocal performance. After tracking a few takes, they are reviewed, and the best parts are moved to the "comp" track. If you identify issues that still require correction, the vocalist will rerecord those parts, and the recordist will insert them into the comp track.

To maintain the performance consistency, entire phrases are performed as you create a comp. For instance, if the line is "Oh say can you see," and "can" is flat, the vocalist would re-sing that entire line in order to fix the single word "can" (rather than just that one word in isolation). The advantage is that the entire line will feel smooth and unedited. The disadvantage is that the vocalist might perform some of the other words inconsistently or incorrectly, with a different timbre or volume, or even breathing rhythmically in a different place, which could spiral into even more corrective work. However, using this approach gives you the option to use either the entire re-performed phrase, or pieces of it, to comp into the keeper.

Note that there are both non-destructive editing (the DAW default setting) and destructive editing (which was the case back in the days of analog recording on tape). *Non-destructive* editing means as you comp, the original files aren't altered in any way. After editing a file, you can "undo" and/or still recall a previous recording. *Destructive* editing means the original files are altered or deleted permanently. You can set your DAW to use destructive editing by selecting one of the available record, punch, or editing modes. This method avoids creating a huge batch of rerecorded takes that you then have to choose from. It forces you to make a decision about which takes are keepers as you go along. This can be a big time saver.

PUNCH-IN APPROACH

The punch-in approach is a classic comping technique that isolates a small phrase or word to rerecord. You punch-in to an existing performance on the same track to modify the offending word or phrase, and then punch out. To do a punch-in effectively, the vocalist should perform with the track using matching emotional energy to what has already been recorded. Here are two common ways to punch-in: manual and automated.

A manual punch-in comp. In our example, the vocalist sings "Oh say can you see." Using the DAW's transport, you punch-in manually just before "can" and punch out just before "see"—in real time, and on the same track. This is common in analog recording and is destructive editing. Digital recording allows you to do the same thing non-destructively.

An automated punch-in comp. Your DAW can do punch-ins and outs for you automatically. In our example, set in and out points using the transport around the word "can." The playback begins one or two measures before the punch-in point (labeled in some DAWs as "pre-roll"). The vocalist sings the whole phrase, and the DAW punches in just before the word "can" and punches out just before "see," also in real time on the same track.

As you go along, pay close attention to the vocalist's phrasing so your recording is seamless. This is because punching in and out can sometimes result in an inconsistent performance. For example, reference Bruno Mars' vocal punch-in on Mark Ronson's "Uptown Funk" (2014). Can you hear when Bruno says "'cause Uptown Funk's gonna give it to you," (0:56), the punched-in repeat of that phrase (1:00) has a totally different emotional energy? Even though it was not seamless, the producer still chose it—and it works!

Playlist approach. Another way to comp is to use the playlist approach, which is also a non-destructive method. Rather than punching into an existing track, in the playlist approach, you record the entire line of the offending phrase multiple times on different tracks. You create a main track that contains the edit choices from the other multiple takes. Four to seven new performances are more than enough. You then mute the word(s) or phrase(s) you want to fix on the main track you're fixing. You take the preferred words or phrases from each new performance, and insert them one at a time into the muted spaces—without replacing or deleting any of the previous performances. When done well, this approach is another seamless way to correct a vocal performance.

Figure 8.1 shows a vocal comp playlist. Six tracks below the top track show each full recorded performance

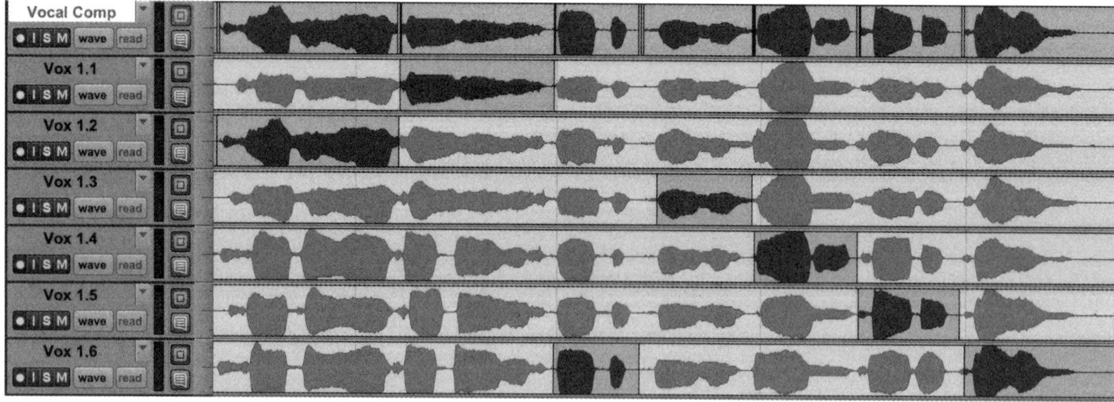

FIG. 8.1. Vocal Comp Playlist (top track)

In figure 8.2, this view of the vocal comp track and the six performances shows only the edited pieces that were used in the comp made from the six takes.

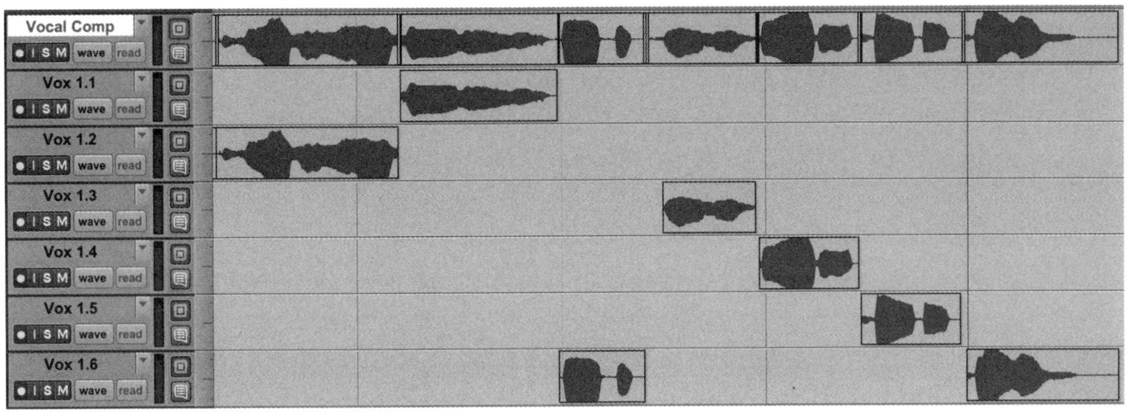

FIG. 8.2. Vocal Comp Playlist: Edited Pieces Only

PITCH CORRECTION

Once your vocal has been comped, it should contain most of the emotion and energy that you will need for your song. If there are still pitch issues, there are great plug-ins that allow you to alter pitch within your performance.

Plug-ins that affect pitch compare the intonation of the vocal performance against a pitch-grid, using the tempered (twelve-tone) scale. You can use these plug-ins to fine-tune the vocal loosely or tightly as desired.

Real-time pitch correction. Pitch can be detected and *quantized* (shifted on the grid) in real time, while the vocalist is performing. This is the hallmark of plug-ins like Antares' Auto-Tune and Waves' Waves Tune. You can vary the speed of the quantization to achieve pitch correction that sounds natural (20 ms or more). The speed adjustment determines how soon the correction moves the note toward the pitch center. Or, you can use real-time pitch correction aggressively to sound more artificial (0 to 20 ms). The vocalist hears the pitch correction playing back as they perform, and it's heard during playback, but the correction is usually not recorded. The aggressive technique was first used by Cher's producers on the song "Believe" (1998), audible in the first verse on the line, "and I can't break through." The artist T-Pain later popularized the technique throughout his entire performance of "I'm Sprung" (2005). Real-time tuning ("autotune") is used in a high percentage of contemporary music, even when the vocalist doesn't need pitch correction, because it lends a sonic EQ characteristic to vocal performances in modern popular music styles.

Offline pitch correction. Another way to alter pitch is by editing it offline (not in real time) using a graph after the vocalist has recorded. With the graphical approach, the X axis is time and the Y axis is pitch. With most offline pitch correctors you can adjust the pitch center, vibratos (pitch modulation), subtle scoops (pitch drift), volume (amplitude), and also shift the resonant frequencies (formants). There are many offline pitch corrector plug-ins on the market, including Celemony Melodyne and Logic's Flex Pitch.

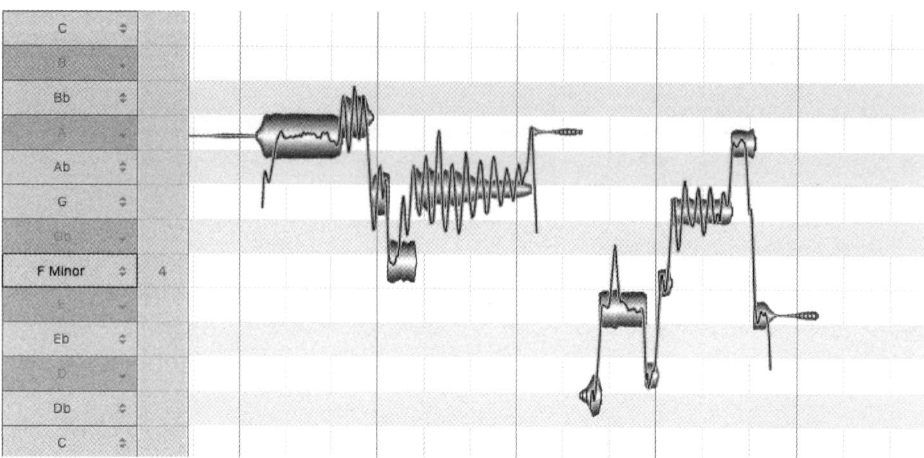

FIG. 8.3. Unedited Vocal Performance with Pitch Modulation and Pitch Drifts Intact. View of the original performance where some pitches are slightly above or slightly below a pitch row.

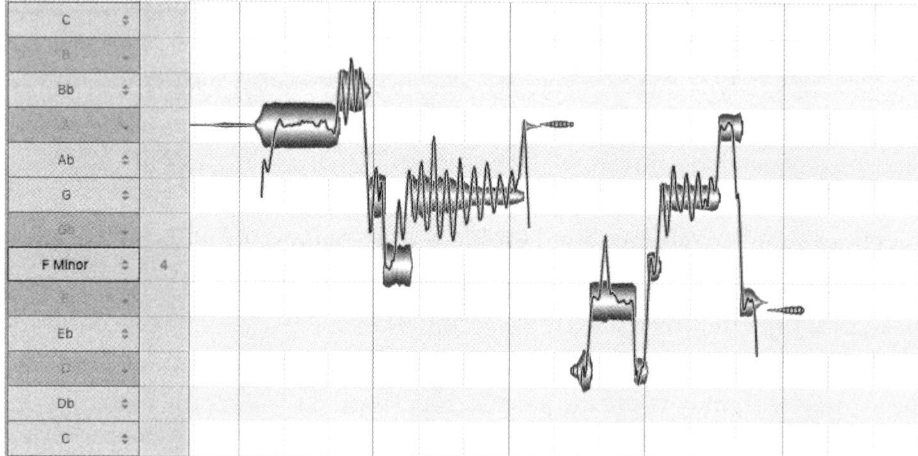

FIG. 8.4. Pitch Quantized Vocal Performance with Natural Pitch Modulation and Pitch Drifts Intact. View of a natural sounding correction where each pitch is centered on a pitch row.

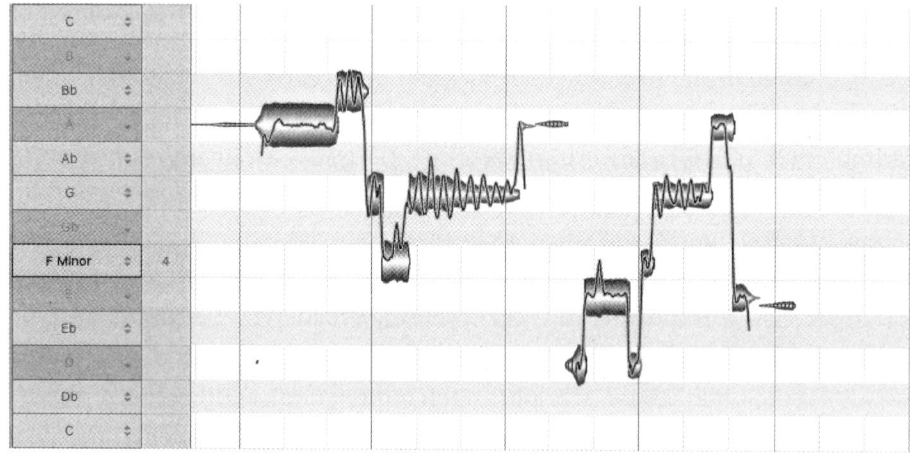

FIG. 8.5. Pitch Quantized Vocal Performance with Edited Pitch Modulation and Pitch Drifts. View of a natural sounding correction where each pitch is centered on a pitch row and the modulation within the note has been lessened.

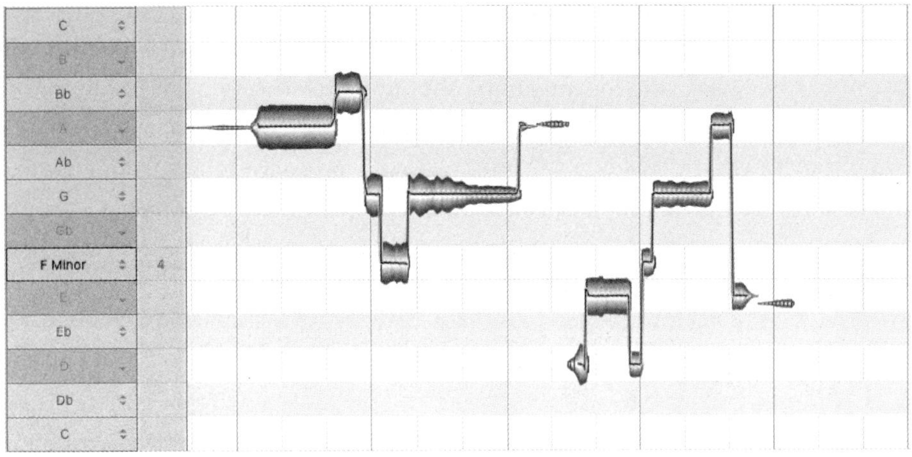

FIG. 8.6. Pitch Quantized Vocal Performance with Flattened Pitch Modulation and Flattened Pitch Drift. View of an artificial sounding correction where the pitch modulation heights have been flattened to create a more robotic sound.

MIDI pitch correction. A MIDI controller can be used to send pitch commands to the tuning plug-in. When the MIDI option is selected on the plug-in, it receives note commands from the MIDI controller as data. Using your controller, you can change the pitch of the note that will be heard from the output of the plug-in. Izotope's Vocal Synth and Antares' Auto-Tune both contain this function.

Between the power and flexibility of your DAW coupled with the right plug-in, you can dial in the right pitches in your vocal performances. What you cannot dial in is the inherent emotion provided by your vocalist. At least, we can't do that yet.

59

Track 59 presents a phrase first sung in tune, then sung again out of tune. The out-of-tune phrase is then adjusted by automatic pitch correction, followed by a graphically (manually) tuned version of the same performance. You can hear in the automatically tuned version that the quantization has also affected the timing. Let's address that also.

TIME CORRECTION

When a vocal performance has been executed well with amazing emotional impact—but is slightly out of time—the first option is always to record it again with better timing, while matching the emotional content of the out-of-time performance (see "Comping" earlier in this chapter). Hopefully, you are successful with this method. But, if you can't get that magic back and want to keep the performance, there are editing options that enable you to adjust timing without rerecording the vocal. We'll need to know the tempo of the song for the most efficient way to adjust the vocal timing.

"Tempo" refers to the number of beats that are counted in a minute (bpm). It is the speed of the music, and what a metronome keeps track of. Time is used to measure the length between beats (how long it takes to get from one beat to another). When tempo fluctuates, the length of time between each beat will vary. Even when musicians play against a metronome, their tempo may shift—sometimes slightly, sometimes drastically

So, before you make any time corrections, you need to know the tempo of your song. While many DAWs default to 120 bpm (beats per minute), of course, songs are played in different tempos. Your DAW tempo can be set before you record the song or can be detected after some recording has been done. Either way, the main display that shows bar, beat, and tick positions should match the song for precise editing.

If you created the music, you know the tempo, and can line yourself up to the bar/beat indicators that should be running vertically on each track within your session. But, what do you do if you have received a piece of music from another songwriter, or are working with an acoustic guitar piece that was recorded without a click? You need to find the tempo.

DETECTING TEMPO

There are a few ways to figure out what tempo (or tempos) a song has, when you haven't set it yourself.

tap tempo A manual way to find the tempo is to do a *tap tempo*. Many DAWs contain this feature. You tap quarter notes as the song plays using a key on your computer, and the DAW detects and displays your average bpm.

bpm counter An automatic way to find the tempo is to use a bpm counter. Some DAWs contain this as a plug-in that detects transient energy, which is produced by peaks in percussive sounds. A bpm counter detects the length of time between beats and displays your average bpm.

Those methods are good for a quick solution, but may not be the most accurate for a song that was performed without a click and you don't know the precise tempo yet. This is because there will be inherent tempo fluctuations in a live performance.

tempo mapping Many DAWs have a feature that will allow the DAW to accurately detect the tempo of your audio, also using transient energy. This changes the DAW's tempo ruler to match the bpm of the recording. This feature is called "tempo mapping" or "beat-mapping." This feature is not common to all DAWs, so you may want to consult your user manual.

Tempo mapping improves your workflow for a session with an unknown bpm. Mapping the tempo provides:

1. an accurate click track for sections of the song that may not contain instruments for the vocalist to follow
2. an accurate count of bars and beats for punches, comps, and moving entire sections of vocals or instruments
3. an easier way to jump to an overdub or editing location using the "go-to" command
4. a grid indicator that can be used for shifting and/or quantizing vocal performances

Once you have your session fully mapped, you can use the map as a fluctuating grid, giving you a vertical indicator for each bar and beat in your song. With that information, it is much easier to change the timing of a performance.

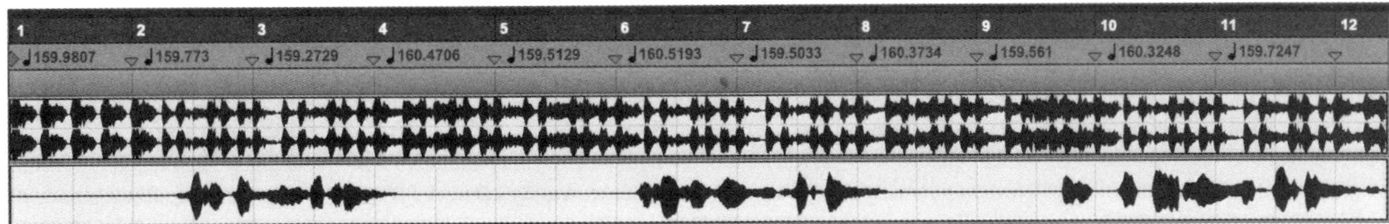

FIG. 8.7. 12-Bar Section of a Song. This shows a fluctuating tempo that is mapped one bar at a time.

MOVING YOUR VOCAL

Cut and Move

Cutting the audio and moving it is useful when you want to nudge the bar/beat position slightly of a selection from the vocal performance. This is a valuable tool to keep a vocal that has a great vibe but is not quite in time. It is also useful for those who are skeptical about potential artifacts that might occur from using a time-stretching method like warping (discussed later this chapter). No distortions will occur when you just use cut and move. A crossfade—overlapping the end of one audio piece with the beginning of the next—might be necessary when you cut and move, to help the smooth the transition between edited pieces.

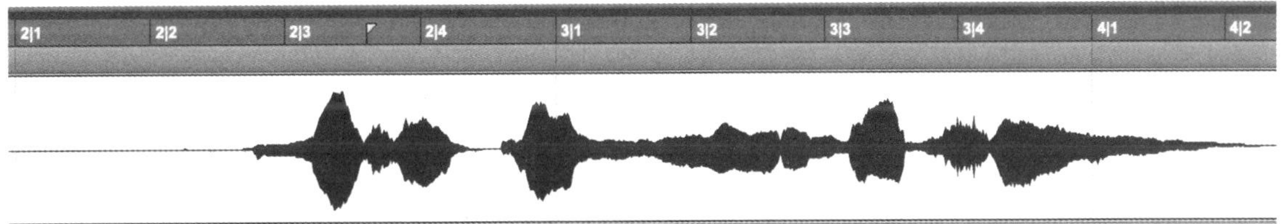

FIG. 8.8. Unedited Vocal Performance, with Second Phrase Slightly Early at Bar 3

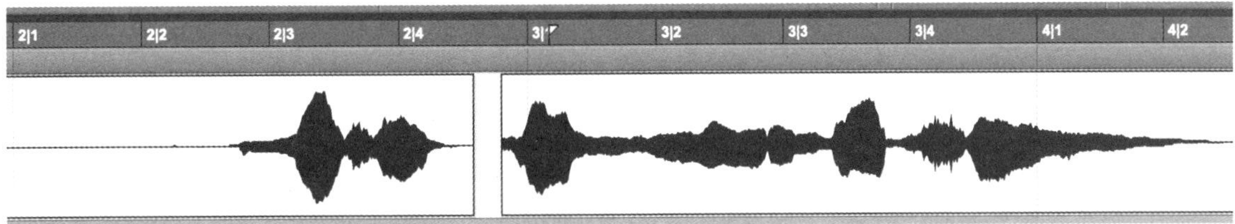

FIG. 8.9. Edited Vocal Performance, with Second Phrase Shifted to Bar 3

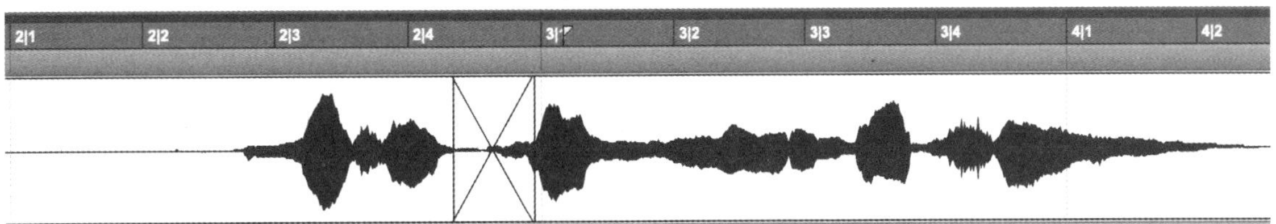

FIG. 8.10. Edited Vocal Performance, with a Crossfade at Bar 3.

Copy (or Cut) and Paste

Copy and paste are useful when you have two sections in your song that are similar enough to replace one with the other. Let's say your emotional content at the beginning of chorus 1 was so good that you want to use it again on the beginning of chorus 2, because you just can't replicate the magic in that performance. Because you know the bar/beat relationship of the two sections, this can be a simple and useful editing technique. Listen once again to Bruno Mars on "Uptown Funk." The consistency of chorus 1 (0:50) and chorus 2 (2:05) is the result of the same performance being copied and pasted.

Time Compression and Expansion (TCE)

When your audio has been performed at varying tempos—for example, chorus 1 is at 120 bpm, but chorus 3 is at 127 bpm—you can move your audio from chorus 1 to chorus 3, and TCE will compress it correctly to align with chorus 3's tempo of 127 bpm.

TCE detects transient energy information in the vocal file, and assigns it a bar/beat position. The bar/beat position then can move with small adjustments to change the timing of the vocal performance. This is useful when moving audio phrases away from each other, without adding spaces that need crossfades. In most basic vocal production scenarios, the timing of your original performance and your edited performance will not be far enough away to hear any unwanted artificial artifacts.

Warping

Warping detects small transient spikes of audio in your vocal performance and assigns those transients to a Bar/Beat position relative to your DAW's tempo or timeline. Once you have enabled a warping mode, your vocal can seamlessly time-stretch and tempo-synchronize (slower, faster, or anything in between). This is an extremely useful tool to quickly move vocals between two similar sections that have differing tempos. You can also warp within a small range, as in moving a single word, or warp a phrase or an entire song. Warping will actually stretch your audio at the sample level, and the changing of tempo is difficult to detect, when done well. Stretching audio does have the potential to add unwanted digital artifacts, but the benefits can outweigh the drawbacks when blended into your song efficiently.

60

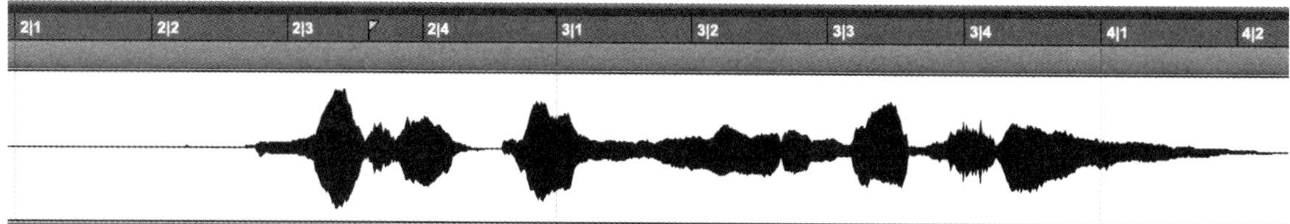

FIG. 8.11. Unedited Vocal Performance, with Second Phrase Slightly Early at Bar 3

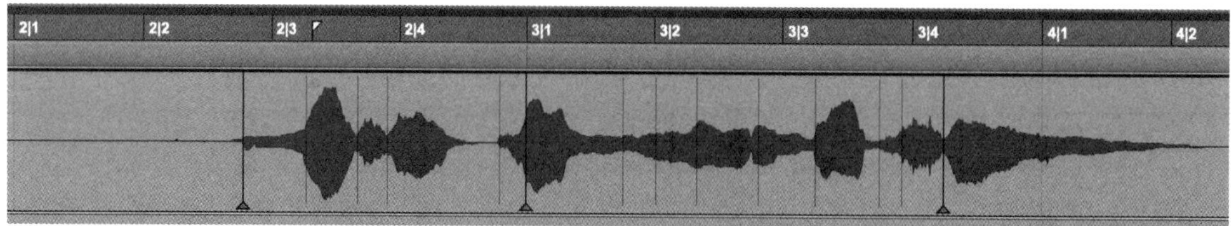

FIG. 8.12. Edited Vocal Performance, with Second Phrase Shifted to Bar 3 Using TCE

WORKING WITH BREATH SOUNDS

As you are comping and editing with your DAW, it is possible to exaggerate, minimize, or delete breath sounds. This is a creative choice. In Michael Jackson's performance of "Thriller," you hear breaths and grunts used throughout as energetic, rhythmic devices.

If your choice is to minimize an extra vocal sound, you can isolate it by separating the breath from the word using your cut editing tool before and after it. You would then use a volume tool to lower the level of the sound. This can also be done with volume automation, in which you lower the level of the vocal sound only at the desired location, without affecting the overall level of the performance.

If you want to exaggerate the sound, instead, you would use the same process to select the sound, but then raise the level.

If you want to eliminate the sound altogether you can just delete it, and use a crossfade for a smooth beginning of the word with the now-deleted breath.

Now that you've finished recording and editing your vocal performance, it's time to mix it so that it can be showcased.

CHAPTER 9

Mixing Vocals

If you have gotten this far in the book, you probably understand enough to create an interesting recording that features a vocalist. In addition to the detail you put into the recording process, your work might not be completed until it is mixed and possibly mastered.

Mixing is the process of blending all the recorded vocal and instrumental tracks into a mix master. The *mix master* is the final mono, stereo, or multi-channel surround product that your audience hears. The final mix master can then be delivered directly to the consumer (uploaded to streaming and other online services, or physical media such CDs and vinyl), or to a mastering engineer for additional processing prior to distribution.

Listening to music through different monitors affects the subjective sound impression for each person. Recording studios use large monitors, mid-field monitors, near-field monitors, small monitors, and headphones at varying levels, to objectively review the frequency response of the mix in progress.

SPL (Sound Pressure Level) is a logarithmic scale used to measure sound. Figure 9.1 illustrates a range of sound pressure levels from quiet to damaging. The National Institute for Occupational Safety and Health (NIOSH) recommends that exposure to sound should be controlled below a level equivalent to 85 dB for 8 hours to minimize hearing loss. It can be useful to use a phone or computer app that measures the SPL in your mixing space for sustainable monitoring exposure.

NOISE LEVEL IN SPL	SOUND SOURCE	EXPOSURE LIMITS WITHOUT EAR PROTECTION	LISTENING LEVELS IN THE STUDIO
SPL levels that cause damage:			
140 dB	Aircraft carrier deck, fireworks, custom car stereo system, gunshot	0 minutes	0
130 dB	Jet taking off, jackhammer	0 minutes	0
120 dB	Rock concert, car horn, emergency siren	0 minutes	0
SPL levels that cause pain:			
109 dB	Concert, sporting event, max output of Apple AirPods	Less than 2 minutes	Max level in studio (engineer wears earplugs!)
106 dB	Personal music player at max volume, hair dryer	3.75 minutes	
103 dB	Motorcycle (while sitting on it)	7.5 minutes	
100 dB	School dance	15 minutes	
97 dB	Lawnmower	30 minutes	
SPL levels that are considered moderately safe with minimum exposure:			
94 dB	Electric drill, power tools	1 hour	Loud level in studio
91 dB	Shouting, motorcycle at 25 feet	2 hours	
88 dB	Food blender	4 hours	
SPL levels that are considered safe:			
85 dB	Vacuum cleaner	8 hours	Comfortable level in studio
55 dB	Normal conversation, air conditioning, background music	Safe	

FIG. 9.1. Sound Levels and Safety

Mixing is an art and a science that is meant to reveal the best intentions of your song. Since vocals are usually the primary feature of vocal-centric projects, knowing how to mix vocals is an important part of any producer's or mixer's skill set. Spending too much time on the instruments and not enough time on the vocals is a common mixing mistake.

Here are five useful aspects of mixing that allow for effective vocal presence in your project:

- level: how quiet or loud
- panorama: how narrow or wide
- equalization: how dull or bright
- dynamic processing: how dynamically sparse or dense
- time-based effects: how close or distant

Yes, these are the same components you used for recording and editing. During the mixing process, you are using these tools to put a finishing shine on your work. Let's take a look.

LEVEL

The most important part of mixing is relative loudness level. The level of a vocal track will always be relative to the instruments in the project. A vocal performance sung against a single piano should sound just as robust as a vocal with a full instrumental production. Reference Adele's vocal level in "Someone Like You" (2011) against the Weeknd's vocal level in "Blinding Lights" (2020). While both vocal performances are distinctly louder than their instrumentation, the mixes are well-balanced—even though Adele's song has a single piano and the Weeknd's song has a full complement of synthetic instruments. Each instrument in the mix has a level that it was recorded at, and its playback level can be changed with each channel's fader. The mixer (mixing engineer) raises or lowers each instrument and vocal level in the mix to create an artistic use of the various recorded parts in the project. Ultimately, the mix master contains the desired level balance of each track for your finished project.

To achieve a distinct and "in front" vocal mix, first monitor the master output meter in your DAW. This is important to get an overall sense of how elevated your overall output levels are when you begin. The output level of a DAW works well when the peak levels of your entire mix (vocals and instrumentation) are -6 to 0 dBFS. If you operate above this level, it can sound good; however, it could also result in unwanted distortion from fast transients (see chapter 6) that overload your mixing output. And if you keep turning things up, eventually your entire mix will distort. This is a common mistake.

Mix Level Strategy Example

Here is a mixing strategy to set overall levels. Go to the spot in the song that has the most information playing. Imagine a song with a full band—drum set, bass guitar, keyboards, electric guitar, horns, strings, percussion, lead vocal, and background vocals. Start with all instrument fader levels at -40 dBFS. You'll hear the entire song, but the master fader output level is very low.

In figure 9.2, instrument tracks are set to -40 dBFS, with a low master fader output level. The LED column in the master fader (at right) displays digital metering. This is the overall output level for the mix master and what is sent to your monitors. The right number LED column in tracks 1-4 display the recorded signal levels. The left number column in each track, including the master fader, is the output level for each fader.

FIG. 9.2. Instrument Tracks Set to –40 dBFS, with Low Master Fader Output Level

Now, bring up the fader level of the kick (bass) drum until the master fader meter registers -16 dBFS. Then, bring up the fader level of the bass guitar to blend with the kick drum. This establishes the low-frequency information in the song. Then, bring up the fader level of the snare drum to complement the kick drum and bass. Finally, raise the fader level of the lead vocal to make sure it is as loud as—but preferably louder than—the other three instruments. These four instruments usually occupy the center of the stereo field; they are the focal points of your mix, and are best represented when the master fader output is registering -6 dBFS to -3 dBFS.

FIG. 9.3. Kick, Snare, Bass, and Lead Vocal Fader Levels Raised to a desired balance in the mix. The overall output level for the mix master displays a peak level of –6 dBFS.

The next thing to blend in are your main pad instruments (guitars, pianos, synthesizers, and background vocals) until they are discernible, but not overwhelming your lead vocal. Add in your hi-hat, snaps, claps, percussion, and other instruments until they are also discernible, but not affecting the relationship of the kick, bass, snare, vocal, and pads. Before you know it, you have a song that is sounding ready for a playlist. Your mix has passed the first step and is now ready for more highlights.

PANORAMA

As we discussed in chapter 5, *panorama* refers to the position of your recorded audio within the stereo field. Any vocal or instrument can occupy the left, center, right, or in-between positions in the stereo field. Panorama is the umbrella term for two concepts. One is panning, in which a mono signal is moved within the stereo field using a potentiometer (pan pot). The other is balance, in which the left and right of a stereo signal (such as two microphones for a choir) can be adjusted separately to widen or narrow their positions in the stereo field.

A mono vocal (or instrument) can pan to any position with the stereo field: from 8 o'clock (the left panning position, to 4 o'clock (the right panning position), and anything in between. When the word "panning" is used, it refers to the stereo field placement of a mono instrument.

FIG. 9.4. Clock Face Reference for Panning (set at 12 O'clock)

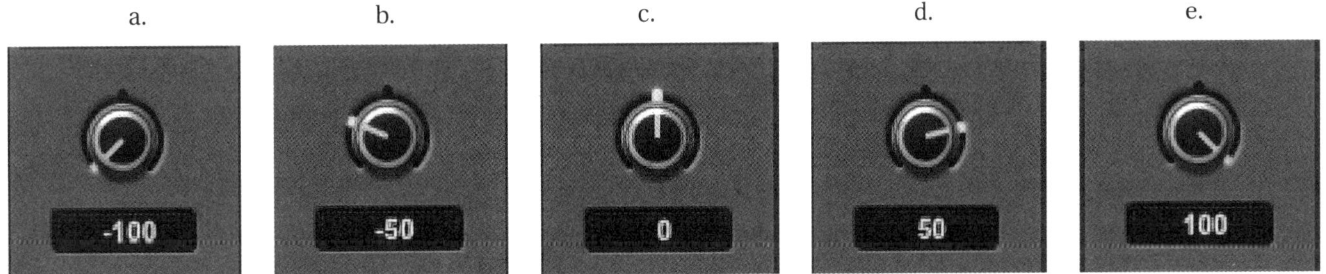

FIG. 9.5. Panning with a Mono Pan Pot (Potentiometer): (a) Left (8 o'clock), (b) slightly left (9:30), (c) center (12 o'clock), (d) slightly right (2:30), and (e) right (4 o'clock)

The center of the stereo field (12 o'clock) is the location of the lead vocal. This will be constant in a large body of your work. This position serves as the best place to drive the energy of your song. Will you get bored and want to place the vocal in different positions from time to time? Possibly, but for the majority of your songs, the lead vocal will be positioned in the center of your stereo field imaging for a well-balanced mix.

61

Doubles of the lead vocal, and harmonies to the lead vocal, also reside pretty close to the center. A slight offset to 11 o'clock or 1 o'clock can be helpful because it allows the lead vocal its own localized position in the center of the stereo field. Each voice in a duet could have various panning positions, from both in the center, to one slightly or completely left, and the other slightly or completely right, based on artistic choices.

Background vocals can be panned to the extreme left and extreme right for a wide image that is useful for choirs, for example. Multiple background vocals can also be cascaded, which would place them in several localized positions. An example would be a vocal at 8 o'clock and its unison at 4 o'clock. The next harmony would be at 9 o'clock and its unison at 3 o'clock. Followed by the last harmony at 11 o'clock and its unison at 1 o'clock.

62

The other concept under the umbrella of panorama is balance. You balance an audio file that has been recorded in stereo. This is most applicable when recording larger vocal ensembles, like choirs. With balance, the left and right panning can vary from the extreme edges to more narrow positioning. Or you can balance the stereo image more to one side or the other by changing the axis of the balance field.

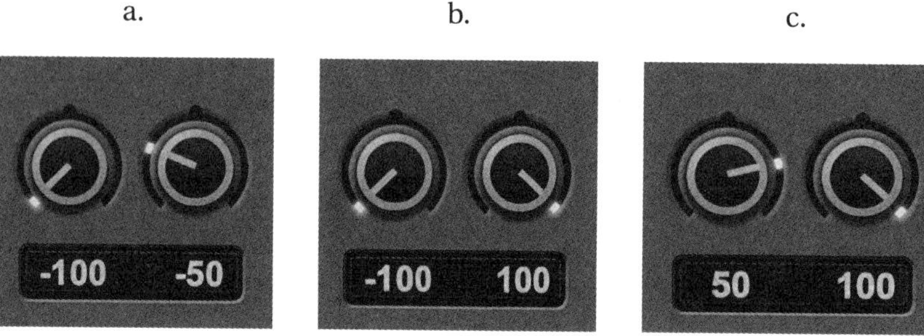

FIG. 9.6. Stereo Tracks Using Two Pan Pots to Balance the Recorded Audio. (a) Stereo image panned mostly left, (b) Stereo image centered (the most common), (c) Stereo image panned mostly right.

EQUALIZERS (EQS)

The human voice can perform as low as 87 Hz and as high as 1,046 Hz, on average. The vast majority of vocal melodies in popular songs fall within the range between notes C3 (130.81 Hz) and C5 (523.25 Hz). Vocal quality is made up of a series of harmonics (different frequency bands, also called overtones) above the fundamental sung pitch (the note you're singing), produced in the vocal tract. These harmonics are what make a voice distinctive. You can alter the recorded quality of the voice by boosting (raising) or attenuating (lowering) the harmonics with equalization.

In your DAW, you use an equalizer (EQ) plug-in for these harmonic adjustments. While there are different types of EQs, *parametric EQ* is the most flexible for fine-tuning your vocal recording. When you boost or attenuate a frequency with a parametric equalizer, a range of frequencies above and below your selected frequency are affected. That range of frequencies is called the *bandwidth*. The width or narrowness of the bandwidth is called the "Q," which stands for "quality." Dividing the center frequency by the bandwidth (the higher frequency above your chosen frequency minus the lower frequency below your chosen frequency) equals Q. Example of Q ranges are .5 (which is pretty wide), 1.5 (which is medium), and 4 (which is narrow).

Equalizers are usually placed "in series" (see chapter 6) across the insert of the track you are processing. There are some critical frequency ranges that might need adjusting for well-balanced mix work.

63

- To manage room rumble and vocal proximity effect, use a high-pass filter with a 12 to 24 dB per octave roll-off at 100 to 150 Hz. Track 63 first presents room rumble being gradually rolled off (60, 120, 180 Hz roll-off at 12 dB octave), and then sung phrases: with room rumble and then with rumble rolled off.

64

- To make a "thin" (treble-heavy) sounding vocal sound more natural, turn 200 Hz up 1 to 3 dB with a moderate Q. Note: this approach can also make a well-recorded vocal sound unattractively "thick" in the low-mid frequencies. Track 64 illustrates a boost at 200 Hz.

65

- To make a harsh-sounding vocal seem less piercing, turn 3 kHz down by 3 to 6 dB with a moderate Q. This works well on mezzo and soprano vocals that are belted in their upper vocal range, for example. Note: this approach may also dull articulation. Listen to track 65.

66

- To emphasize articulation on a dull vocal, turn up 8 kHz by 1 to 3 dB with a moderate Q. Note: this approach also works well on a well-recorded vocal that may still need more clarity. Listen to track 66.

67

- To make a vocal sound present in a mix, yet not too loud, add a bit of "crispness" by raising 11 to 14 kHz by 3 to 6 dB with a narrow Q. Listen to track 67.

Note: increasing frequencies from 7 to 14 kHz can also increase the potential for sibilant "s" syllables, but those can be managed with dynamic processing techniques such as de-essing (discussed later in his chapter).

DYNAMIC PROCESSING

Dynamic processing manages the overall range of levels for your vocal recording. Compressors, limiters, gates, and expanders are the four dynamic processors that you will find in your DAW. Vocalists perform using dynamics (soft and loud volumes) naturally; dynamic processing alters the volumes of the vocal performance artificially.

Dynamic processors are *attenuators*, meaning they turn sound down. Compressors and limiters turn sound down *above* a set threshold. This helps maintain an even dynamic level for the vocal to avoid loud peaks. Gates and expanders turn sound down *below* a set threshold. This helps to eliminate low-level noises that could interfere with the vocal performance. Let's look at common settings for all four processors.

68

compressor Enables you to lower the louder parts of the vocal, using an input to output ratio. While there is no hard and fast rule for compression in mixes (much like using salt and pepper in a meal), the best practice in most styles is to use it minimally: ratios no greater than 4:1 (where 4 is the input and 1 is the output). The threshold indicator displays where the attenuation begins *above* threshold, and the gain reduction indicator displays how much the vocal is being lowered.

Compression sounds the most natural when the gain reduction indicator does not exceed -6 dB. (Refer to chapter 6 for a detailed discussion of compression.) Track 68 shows the effect of compression on a vocal with a wide dynamic range.

69

limiter "Flattens" (remove dynamics) from an audio signal. A limiter is a compressor with a high ratio (10:1 up to infinity:1) that is used in commercial music for a uniform dynamic range, unlike classical music and jazz, for example. Popular music has benefitted from using limiters since the radio broadcasts of the 1930s, and continues to be a broadcasting standard. Again, like compression, limiting sounds the most natural when the gain reduction indicator does not exceed -6 dB. Track 69 shows the effect of limiting on a vocal with a wide dynamic range.

70

gate Removes noise, such as breaths or background sounds in between phrases, by lowering the signal *below* threshold—meaning, as the signal is lowering, the gate lowers it even more. A gate uses a high ratio (also 10:1 up to infinity:1), so when the signal goes below the threshold by 1 dB, the gate lowers it by 9 dB more—for a total of 10 dB lower. Gates were useful in the era of analog tape to limit tape hiss and amp noise. Because digital audio is much quieter than tape, today, gates are used less frequently for corrections and are more often as a creative tool. Track 70 shows how gating can reduce ambient noise.

71

expander Also removes noise, such as breaths or background sounds in between phrases, by lowering the signal *below* threshold using a varying ratio. For example, at a 4:1 ratio, when the signal goes below the threshold by 1 dB, the expander lowers it by 3 dB more—for a total of 4 dB lower. Expanders, which are gates with a more subtle attenuation, don't actually expand the dynamic range—instead, they lower the noise floor. This gives the illusion of a wider, "expanded" range of soft and loud volumes. Track 70 shows how an expander can reduce ambient noise.

72

Sibilance is an exaggerated "s" sound in speech that you may wish to remove, or soften, in a vocal performance (see chapter 7). A de-esser, which is a compressor with two inputs, can accomplish this. Input 1 is the normal compression function. Input 2 is the "side chain" function that exaggerates a small range of frequencies. When the side chain is activated, the compressor no longer responds to input 1. Instead, it responds to input 2, which lowers an exaggerated frequency that you have set. Sibilance happens between 4 and 10 kHz, so you can select a center frequency within that range to attenuate. De-essers sound most natural when the gain reduction does not exceed -3 dB. Too much attenuation can make the vocalist sound like they're lisping. Track 72 shows how a de-esser can reduce sibilance.

A final word about compression and limiting: In some genres, like EDM, producers characteristically flatten the level variations of a vocal performance, to make sure the vocal level sits evenly above the instrumentation. In other genres, like jazz, folk, and classical, producers may prefer to minimize any artificial level alterations in favor of the vocalist's natural performance levels. These are creative choices.

TIME-BASED EFFECTS

Time-based effects—reverbs, delays, phasers, flangers, and chorus—are added to your vocal performance to enhance or reduce its perceived space, distance, complexity, or size.

Reverbs

Reverb gives you a sense of the space the vocalist is in. You will see church, hall, plate, and room reverbs in most of the reverb plug-ins contained within your DAW. A good starting point for vocals is usually a plate reverb because its length and "color" fit across a wide range of tempos.

A good rule of thumb is to use a longer reverb time in slower songs, and a shorter reverb time in faster songs. When your vocalist needs to deliver a long series of rapid lyrics, the articulation will be clearer when the reverb is short.

Decay (i.e., the duration of reverb times) can be timed against the song's tempo. Here is another good rule of thumb: set the decay duration to the length of two beats in your song. To determine the duration of two beats, divide the number of milliseconds (ms) in a minute (60,000) by the song's tempo. That number will be the duration (in ms) of a single beat in your song. Multiply that number by 2, and you will have a great starting point for the plate reverb that you will add to a vocal.

73

Track 73 presents a vocal with the following types of reverb: dry (no reverb), medium digital plate reverb, simulated large hall reverb, and simulated small tight room reverb.

"RT" Reverb Time (Decay) Duration Calculations to Get a Two-Beat Decay			
Song Tempo	**Duration of One Beat**	**Duration of Two Beats**	**Decay Setting**
120 bpm	60,000 ms/120 bpm = **500** ms/beat	500 ms/beat x 2 = **1,000** ms	1,000 ms (1.0 s)
90 bpm	60,000 ms/90 bpm = **666.7** ms/beat	666.7 ms/beat x 2 = **1,333.4** ms	1,333.4 ms (1.3 s)
60 bpm	60,000 ms/60 bpm = **1,000** ms/beat	1,000 ms/beat x 2 = **2,000** ms	2,000 ms (2.0 s)

If you want to be more creative with your vocal mixing, use different spaces that include shorter or longer reverb times by using additional beats or subdividing beats.

The following are default reverb choices within a standard DAW reverb plug-in:

Reverb Default	Duration
Church	4.4 s to 8.7 s
Hall	2.2 s to 4.5 s
Plate	817 ms to 1.6 s
Room	501 ms to 1.0 s
Ambient (Bathroom)	110 ms to 220 ms

Additional reverb parameters can also include:

69 **pre-delay** Sets the amount of time between the original dry sound and the audible perception of the early reflections and reverb time.

high frequency cut Tones down the high frequency information in the reverb to create contrast between the source vocal and the reverb.

low pass filter Contours the low frequency information in the reverb to create contrast between the source vocal and the reverb.

diffusion Defines the number of radiating directions your reverb travels when it hits a reflective surface. A low diffusion usually sounds better on vocals, while a high diffusion usually sounds better on drums.

wet/dry ratio Sets the amount of original signal in relationship with the affected signal. Used by mixers in parallel (see chapter 6) at 100 percent wet so that the original signal sends its information to the reverb on a separate "auxiliary" track.

Delays

Delays give you a sense of distance, as well as complexity and size. Distance in this case is specifically a tempo-based repetition of words or phrases, like an echo. The echo can give the listener the sense of different distances within a large space, such as an auditorium or a stadium. Producers also use delays artistically to repeat the end of a phrase for an arrangement component, which is called "ear candy."

There are three primary elements that you need to adjust when setting up a delay effect:

delay time Sets the amount of time before you hear the delayed audio signal.

feedback Sets how many delay repeats you hear.

wet/dry ratio Sets the amount of original signal in relationship with the affected signal (see reverb above).

While it's easy to use a delay in series across the insert of your vocal track, this setting limits some of the creative functionality by forcing you to use the wet/dry ratio as the volume controller. A better way to use it is in parallel, in which your track's send is the volume controller, and the delay receives the information, in parallel, on a separate aux track.

To use delays creatively, it's best to know your song's tempo. Most plug-in delays allow you to set the delay time to the tempo automatically, by selecting a note duration such as eight notes, quarter notes, half notes, and whole notes. The feedback setting can be set to increase the number of repeats you want.

To set the delay time manually, you can use the 60,000 ms/bpm formula against the bpm of your session. Once you know the duration of a single beat, you can subdivide or multiply by increments of 2 to determine note durations that fit your song. An example is a quarter-note delay at 120 bpm. 60,000/120 = 500 ms (see reverb, earlier in this chapter). You can also subdivide by 3 if you want a triplet duration.

The following audio tracks include an initial untreated recording and then a recording featuring the addition of each effect.

74

A *mono delay* (track 74) will be heard in a single location, which is preferably the center of the stereo field. But it can also be heard on the left, on the right, or anywhere in between; it's your creative choice.

75

A *stereo delay* (track 75) will be heard in the left and right sides of the stereo field, not in the center, like a mono delay. This is useful for left/right panned background vocals, for example, to mirror their placement in the stereo field. One way to achieve this is to use two mono sends, one on the left and one on the right, using the same delay time. This works because there is a natural offset with the separate takes of our background vocals.

Another option is to use a stereo send, which sums the left and right sides together into one mono signal, instead of two separate mono signals. You have to create a stereo illusion with this option, by setting the left and right side delay time settings to be different from one another—otherwise, it will sound like a mono delay. Using our 120 bpm example, to achieve a stereo quarter note delay, set the left side to 495 ms and the right side to 505 ms, rather than both to 500 ms. Note that at any tempo, when using the 60,000 ms/bpm formula, this +/–5 bpm offset between the left and right sides achieves a stereo illusion.

76

A *ping-pong delay* (track 76) will occur on one side and then occur on the other side and then return to the first side before going back to the second side again. This can continue as long as you want. Your signal needs to arrive at one side of the stereo field with some duration—say, the left at a duration of 250 ms (an eighth note at 120 bpm). The left now sends its signal to the right, delayed by the same 250 ms (which means you will hear it 500 ms later than the original vocal). The right now sends it back to the left 250 ms later (which is 750 ms later than the original vocal). And the left sends it back to the right 250 ms later (which is 1 second later than the original vocal). A ping and a pong, or a ping and a pong and a ping and a pong, are usually sufficient when using this delay effect. Be sure to set your feedback time to 0 for this to work. With analog signal routing, you would have used two mono delay devices to achieve this effect. However, your DAW may not be able to do so with mono plug-ins. There are stereo plug-ins that are designed specifically for this popular effect.

Phasers

77

Phasers create a copy of your vocal that is treated with an all pass filter. The filter creates a series of slightly out-of-phase peaks and troughs that can be heard as a resonant frequency. Changing the blended copy's ratio to the original audio creates a shifting of the resonant frequency that we hear as phasing. This is a specialty effect that is used sparingly in vocal productions to create an interesting vocal tension in the song.

Flangers

78

Flangers also create a copy of your vocal. The copy is then added to your original vocal but is slightly delayed, creating a resonant frequency that can move, creating a "sweeping" sound. An LFO (low frequency oscillator) modulates the delay time, from short to long, in an oscillating fashion. The modulation causes the resonant frequency to drop in pitch with a longer delay time, and to rise in pitch with a short delay time—resulting in the sweeping sound. Flanging is a specialty effect used sparingly to create an interesting vocal tension in your composition. One example is the song "Drunk in Love" by Beyoncé, heard on the fourth instance of "love" at the end of the choruses.

Chorus

79

Chorus devices create a copy of your vocal. The copy is then added to your original vocal but is slightly delayed and pitch shifted, which creates a non-harmonically aligned variation of resonant frequencies. An LFO is used to modulate the delay time and pitch with longer delay times and less feedback than a flanger. Chorus devices can be used to make your vocals sound fuller by creating a double-tracking effect.

CONCLUSION

When you listen to music, listen to all kinds of music. Attempt to make your own competitive sounding original versions of what you are hearing. Do not take on too much at first. Try to vocal-produce, and mix, simple songs with only a few instruments, and one vocal at first. Then, build your skills by adding additional vocals and time-based effects as you gain confidence. Your ear for detail will grow over time, and your songs will benefit from the exercises. A great goal is to have songs that are a presentable representation of your work. If you have done that, and it can stand next to other compositions that live competitively in your space, then you have arrived as a vocal producer.

INDEX

ABOUT THE AUTHORS

Jeannie Gagné, M.A. is a professional vocalist, songwriter, pianist, recording artist, author, and educator. She has appeared on TV, award-winning movies, and has toured in Asia, Africa, Europe, South America, and throughout the United States. A songwriter with hundreds of songs to her credit, she appears on dozens of recordings, including her own three critically acclaimed solo albums. She's worked with noted artists such as Philip Glass, Cher, George Duke, comedians/musicians Penn & Teller, and even opened for Bare Naked Ladies. A leading expert in vocal technique and contemporary styles, she has taught tens of thousands of singers for over thirty years to use their voices effectively and authentically in a broad range of styles, using anatomical facts to maximize vocal efficiency, breath management, style, quality, and health. A Professor of Voice at Berklee College of Music in Boston, Massachusetts, she is the author of *Your Singing Voice: Contemporary Styles, Techniques, and Expression* and *Belting: A Guide to Healthy, Powerful Singing* (Berklee Press). She is also the author of Berklee Online's *Popular Singing Styles: Developing Your Sound* course, which she teaches year round. Visit jeanniegagne.com and YouTube.com/TheVocalGenie.

Prince Charles Alexander, M.S. is a multi-GRAMMY winning, multi-platinum producer, mixing engineer, recording engineer, musician, recording artist, songwriter, and educator. His group Prince Charles and the City Beat Band enjoyed a successful run, charting a gold album with Virgin Records in the early 1980s. In the mid 1980s, he moved behind the scenes to produce, record, and mix other artists. His client base would grow to include Mary J. Blige, the Notorious B.I.G., Puff Daddy, Usher, Boyz II Men, Brandy, Babyface, Sting, Aretha Franklin, Donnie McClurkin, and many others. Charles's accolades include more than forty Platinum and Gold certifications from the RIAA, three GRAMMY wins, and seven GRAMMY nominations from the Recording Academy, and a Victoire de la Musique (the French equivalent of a GRAMMY).

Prince Charles is currently an active producer/engineer and professor in the Music Production & Engineering Department at Berklee College of Music in Boston, where he created their Commercial Record Production curriculum, and is a Professor of the Practice at Northeastern University. He is the author of *Hip-Hop Production: Inside the Beats* (Berklee Press), author of Berklee Online's master's level courses *Commercial Vocal Production* and *Genre Survey for Songwriters*, as well as co-author of the popular undergraduate level course, aptly titled *Vocal Production*, which has been running year round since 2015.